World Geography

Columbus, Ohio

Send all inquiries to:
School Specialty Publishing
8720 Orion Place
Columbus, OH 43240-2111

ISBN 0-7696-5506-8

1 2 3 4 5 6 7 8 9 10 POH 09 08

The Globe

Imagine you are flying around in space. You look down and see a big round ball. It is the earth.

A model of the earth is called a globe. It is a round map that shows land and water. It uses colors to show which is the land and which is the water.

Directions: Unscramble the letters below to find out the colors that are used on the globe.

Land is ____________________. e r g e n

Water is ____________________. l u b e

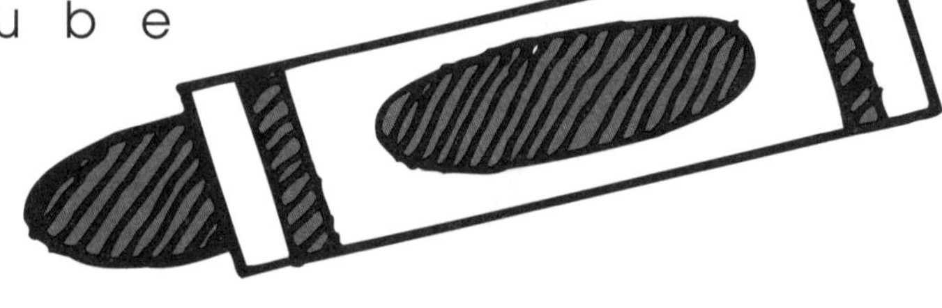

Color the land on the globe green.

Color the water on the globe blue.

It's a Round World

Use these maps with pages 8 and 9.

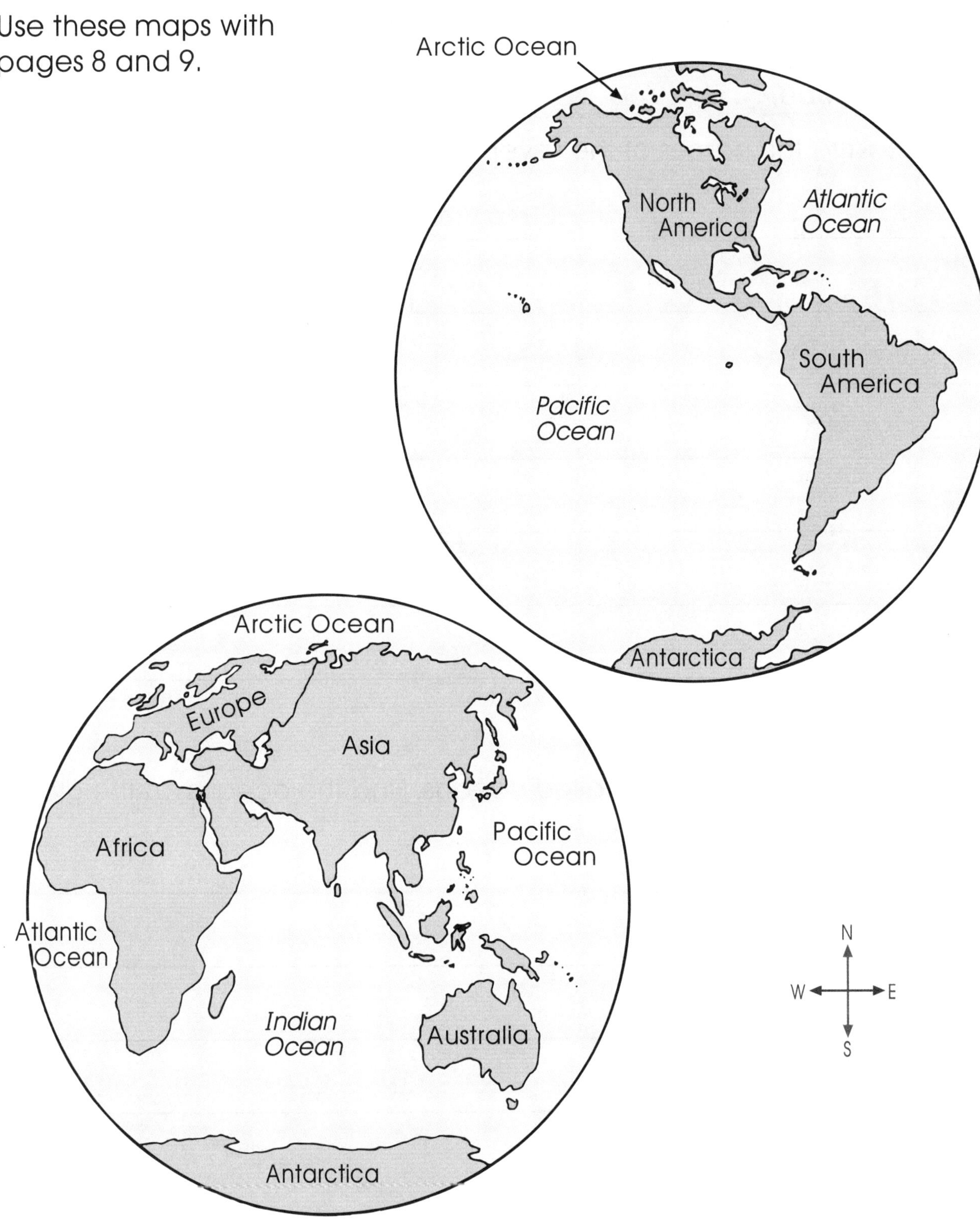

It's a Round World

The picture of the globe on page 7 shows both halves of the world. It shows the large pieces of land called continents. There are seven continents. Find them on the globe.

Directions: Write the names of the seven continents.

1. ______________________________

2. ______________________________

3. ______________________________

4. ______________________________

5. ______________________________

6. ______________________________

7. ______________________________

There are four bodies of water called oceans. Find the oceans on the globe. Write the names below.

1. ______________________________

2. ______________________________

3. ______________________________

4. ______________________________

A Global Guide

Use the globe on page 7. Read the clues below. Write the answers on the lines. Then, use the numbered letters to solve the riddle at the bottom of the page.

1. This direction points up. ____ ____ ____ ____ ____ (1, 2, 22, 3)

2. This direction points down. ____ ____ ____ ____ ____ (4, 5, 6)

3. This direction points right. ____ ____ ____ ____ (7, 8)

4. This direction points left. ____ ____ ____ ____ (9, 10)

5. This ocean is west of North America. ____ ____ ____ ____ ____ ____ ____ (11, 12) ____ ____ ____ ____ ____ (13, 14)

6. This ocean is south of Asia. ____ ____ ____ ____ ____ ____ (15, 16, 17) ____ ____ ____ ____ ____

7. This ocean is east of South America. ____ ____ ____ ____ ____ ____ ____ ____ (18, 19) ____ ____ ____ ____ ____ (20, 21)

Riddle: What does a globe do? ____ ____ (15, 6) ____ ____ ____ ____ ____ (4, 11, 15, 21, 8)

____ ____ (5, 10) "____ - ____ ____ ____ ____ ____" (12 - 22, 2, 5, 21, 16)

____ ____ ____ (13, 5, 22) ____ ____ ____ ____ ____ ____. (11, 19, 14, 17, 7, 18)

Land and Water

Directions: Use the map below plus a wall map to do this activity.

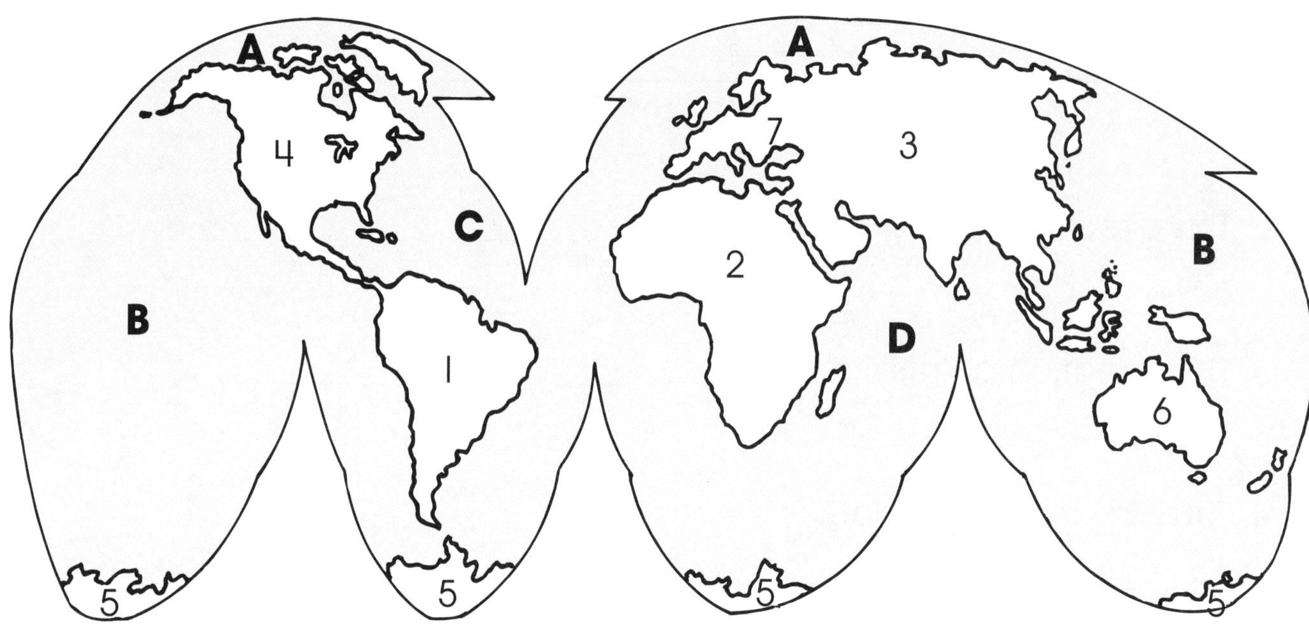

Write the name of each continent in the correct blank.

1. ______________________
2. ______________________
3. ______________________
4. ______________________
5. ______________________
6. ______________________
7. ______________________

Write the name of each ocean in the correct blank.

A. ______________________

B. ______________________

C. ______________________

D. ______________________

Use crayons or markers to follow these directions.

1. Color Australia green.
2. Color Europe yellow.
3. Color Africa orange.
4. Color Antarctica blue.
5. Color North America red.
6. Color South America brown.
7. Color Asia purple.

Color My World

Is it a city, state, country, continent or body of water? Color each box according to the Color Key. Use an atlas for help.

Color Key

city—orange　　state—green　　country—yellow
water—blue　　continent—purple

Atlantic Ocean	India	Colorado	Miami
Peru	Antarctica	Lake Michigan	Hawaii
New Orleans	Spain	Europe	Gulf of Mexico
Vermont	Phoenix	Japan	Paris
East China Sea	Egypt	Wyoming	Sweden
Africa	London	Hudson Bay	Connecticut
Greece	Minnesota	South America	Dallas
Oakland	Great Salt Lake	Argentina	Arctic Ocean
North America	Canada	Chicago	Arkansas
Lake Victoria	Iowa	Asia	Venezuela
Lima	Persian Gulf	Mexico	Moscow
Pacific Ocean	Maryland	Cincinnati	Brazil

Where in the World Is...

What is your global address? It's more than your street, city, state and ZIP code.

What would your address be if you wanted to get a letter from a friend living in outer space?

Use an atlas, encyclopedia, science book or other source to complete your global address.

Inter-Galactic Address Book

Name ______________________________

Street ______________________________

County or Parish ______________________________

State or Province ______________________________

Country ______________________________

Continent ______________________________

Hemisphere ______________________________

Planet ______________________________

Galaxy ______________________________

Draw an **X** to mark the approximate place where you live.

Where in the World?

Refer to the globe on page 7, a real globe or a world map. Find the seven continents and four oceans. Now, you are ready to make your own globe using this page and pages 15 and 17.

Directions:

1. Cut out all the continent and ocean labels.
2. Glue them where they belong in the boxes on the maps on pages 15 and 17.
3. Cut out all of the map circles along the outer lines.
4. Fold each circle in half along the dotted line. Keep the map side on the inside.
5. Be sure to keep the numbers on the circles at the top. Glue the back of the right half of circle **1** to the back of the left half of circle **2**.
6. Glue the back of the right half of circle **2** to the back of the left half of circle **3**.
7. Glue the back of the right half of circle **3** to the back of the left half of circle **4**.
8. Complete the globe by gluing the back of the right half of circle **4** to the back of the left half of circle **1**.

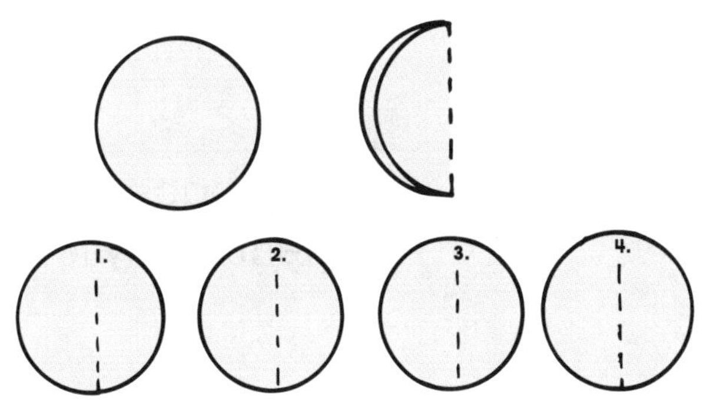

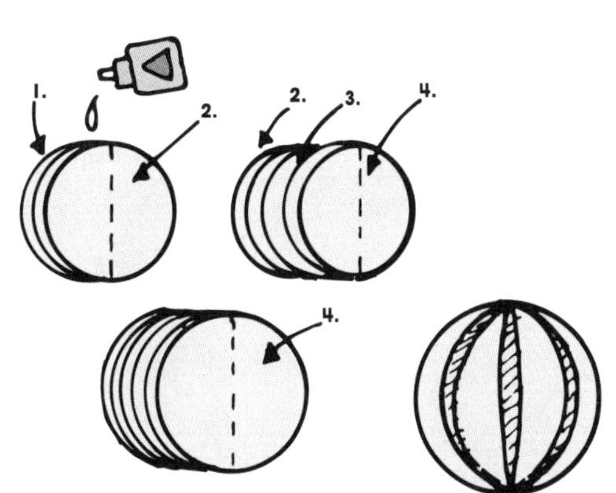

This page has been intentionally left blank.

Where in the World?

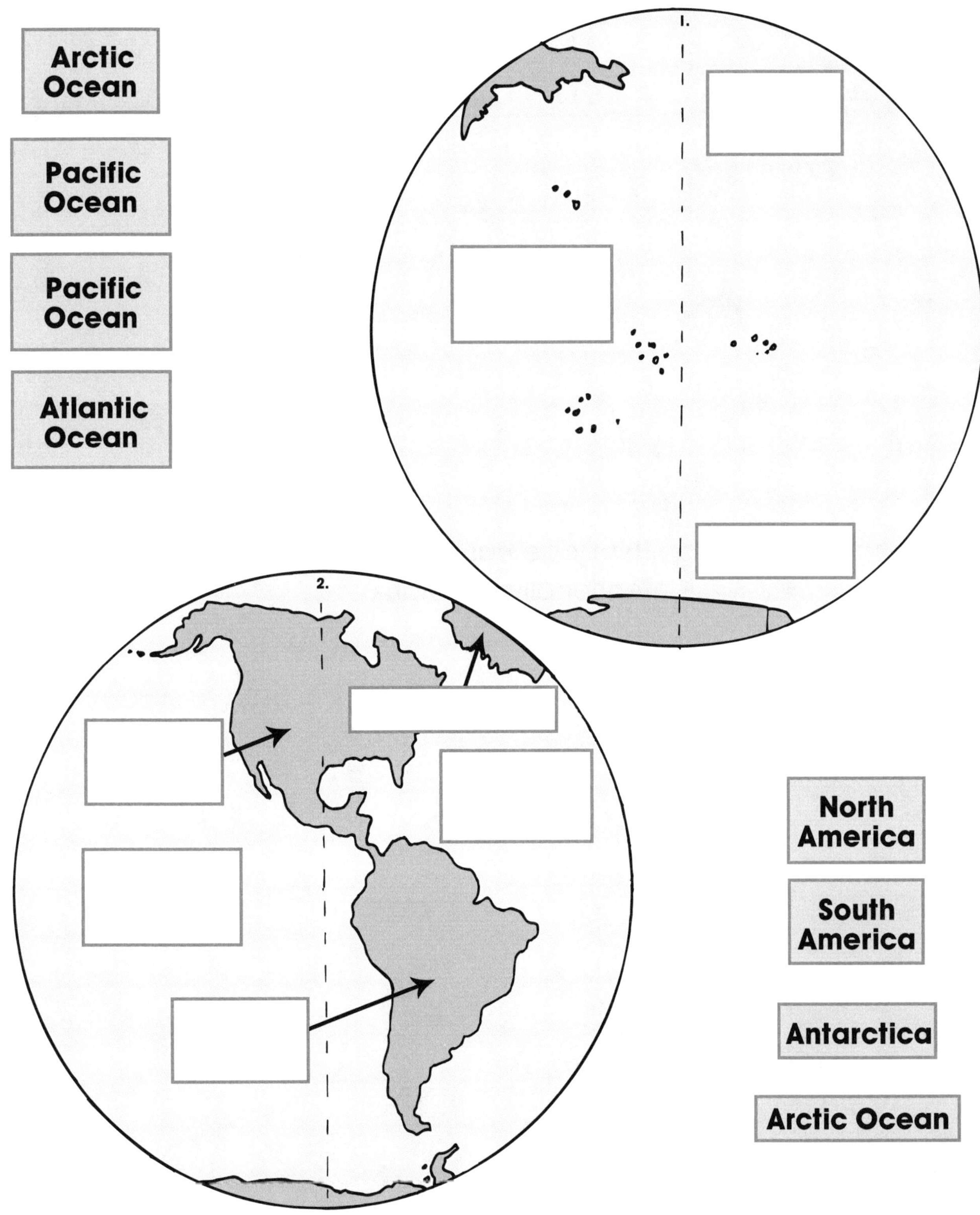

This page has been intentionally left blank.

Where in the World

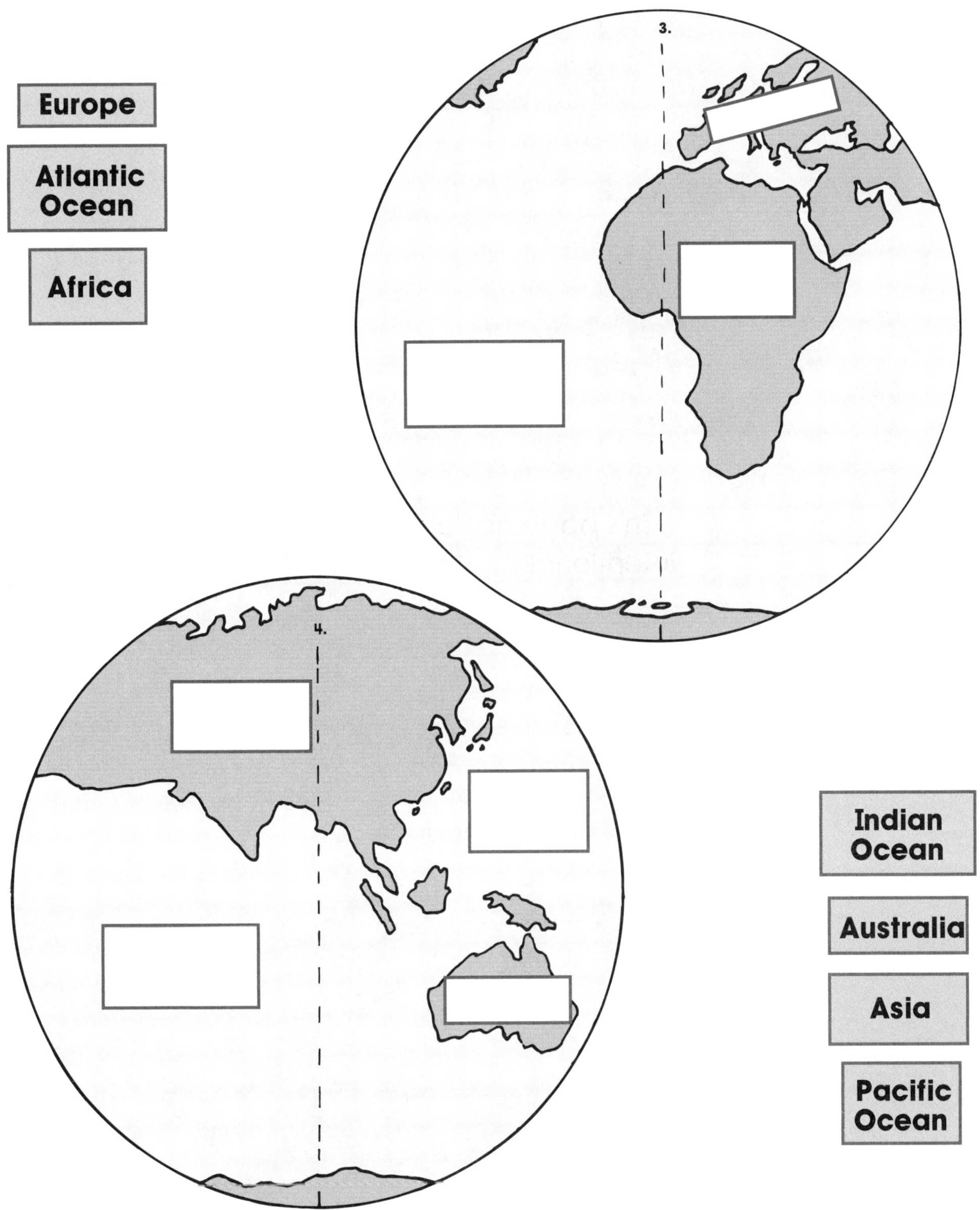

This page has been
intentionally left blank.

Near and Far

Below is a map of the world. It shows the seven continents. Around the map are pictures of animals that are native to the continents. The continent on which each animal can be found is written below the name of the animal.

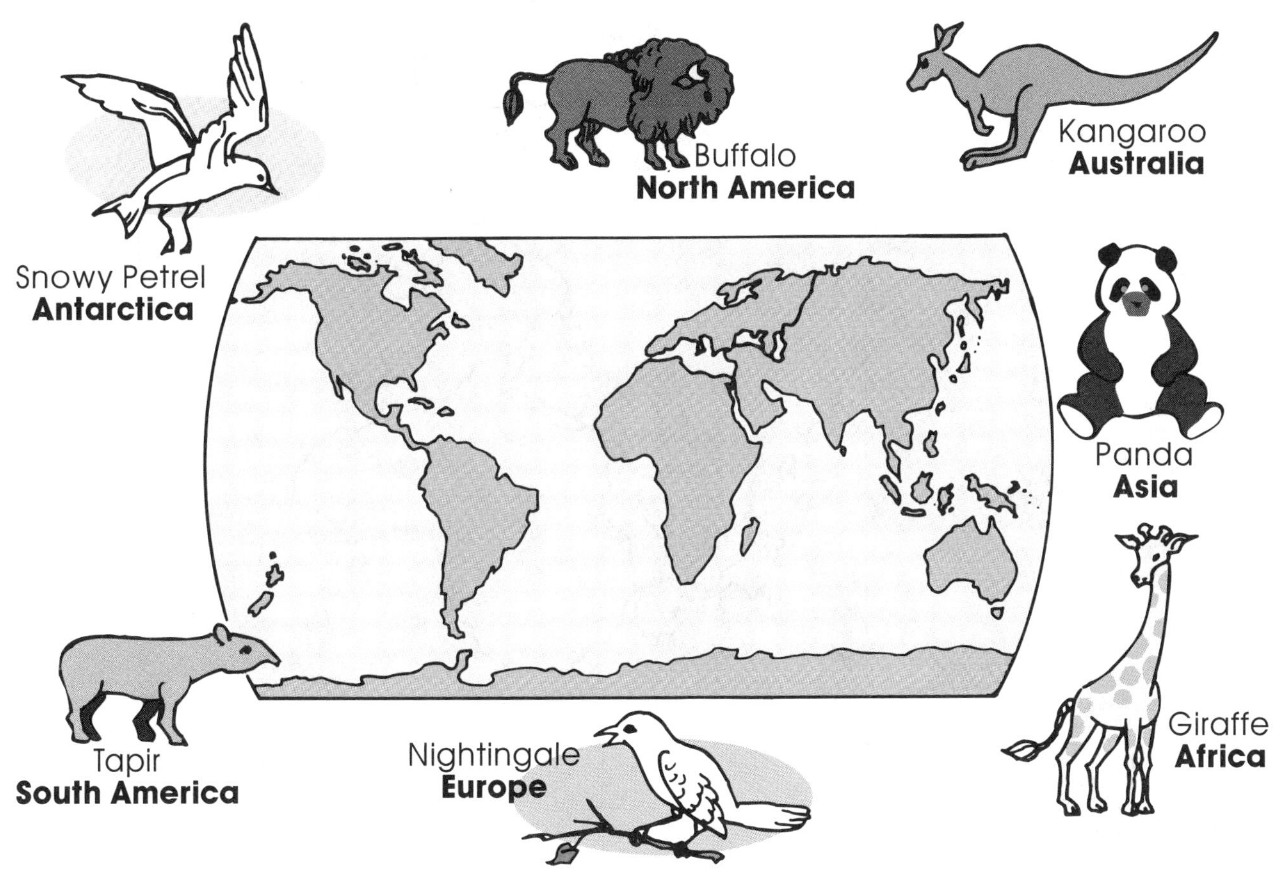

Directions: Use a globe or world map to locate each continent. Draw a line from the picture of the animal to the continent where it is found.

1. Find the continent where you live.

2. Which animal lives on your continent? ______________________

3. Which animal lives on a continent far from you? ________________

Let's Travel the Earth

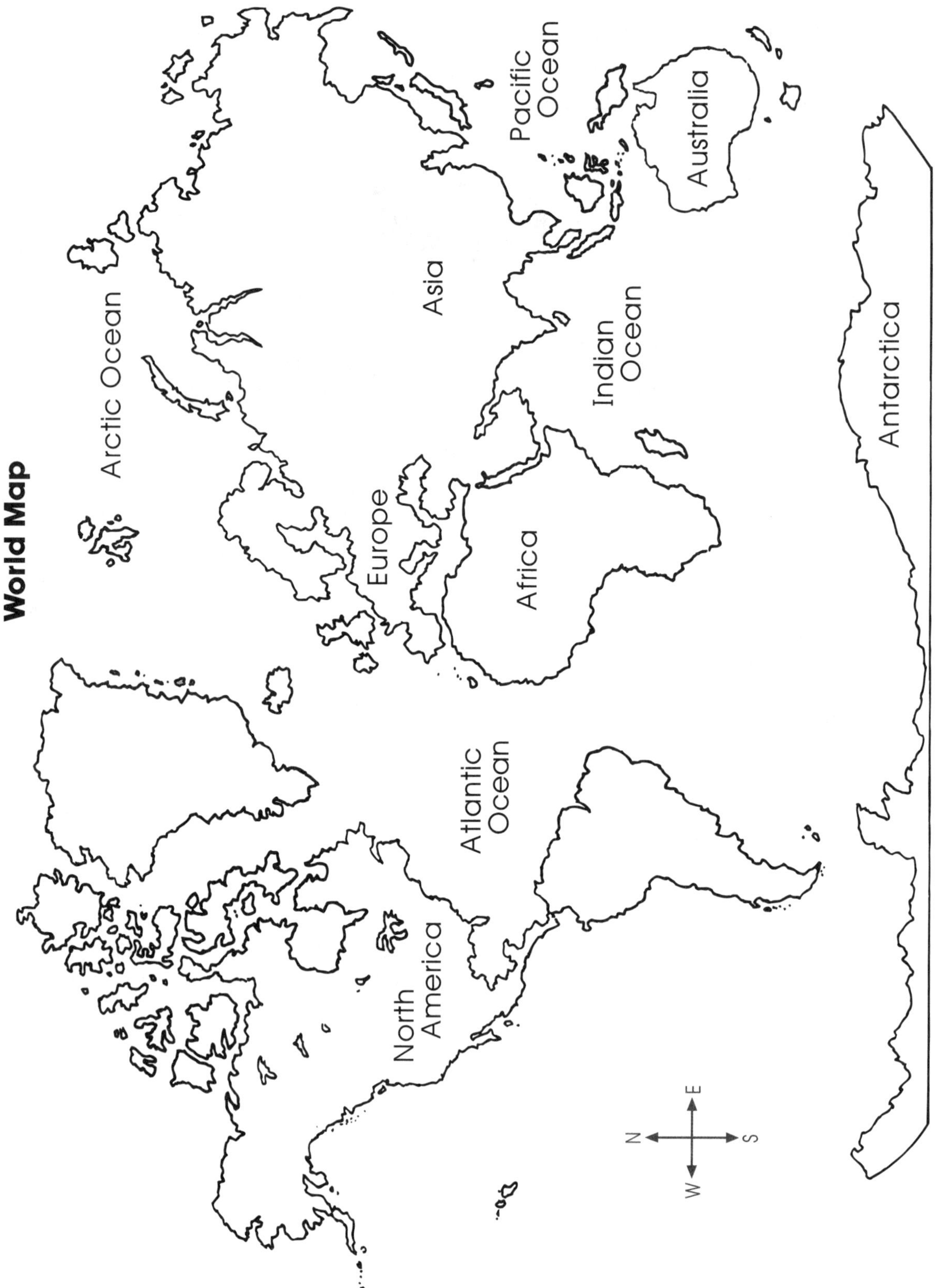

Use with page 21.

Let's Travel the Earth

Directions: Use the map on page 20 to answer the questions below.

Circle the word that correctly completes each statement.

1. If you sail from North America to Antarctica, you will be on the . . .
   Arctic Ocean   Atlantic Ocean   Indian Ocean
2. If you fly from Africa to Australia, you will fly over the . . .
   Indian Ocean   Pacific Ocean   Atlantic Ocean
3. To sail from Europe to South America, you will sail on the . . .
   Pacific Ocean   Arctic Ocean   Atlantic Ocean
4. To sail from North America to Europe, you will sail on the . . .
   Indian Ocean   Atlantic Ocean   Pacific Ocean
5. To travel from Europe to Asia, you must cross . . .
   the Pacific Ocean   the Indian Ocean   land

Fill in the blanks with the correct word.

1. The continent north of South America is ______________________.
2. The ocean directly south of Asia is the ______________________.
3. The ocean directly north of Asia is the ______________________.
4. The continent directly south of Europe is ______________________.
5. The continent directly south of Australia is ______________________.

Use a crayon or marker to follow these directions.

1. Draw a red line from North America to Africa.
2. Draw a green line from Asia to Antarctica.
3. Draw an orange line from Australia to Africa.
4. Draw a black line from Europe to South America.
5. Circle the names of all four oceans with blue.
6. Color North America green.
7. Draw a black dotted line (- - - - - -) around South America.

Hemispheres

The earth is a sphere. When the earth is cut in half horizontally along an imaginary line called the **equator**, the **Northern** and **Southern Hemispheres** of the earth are created.

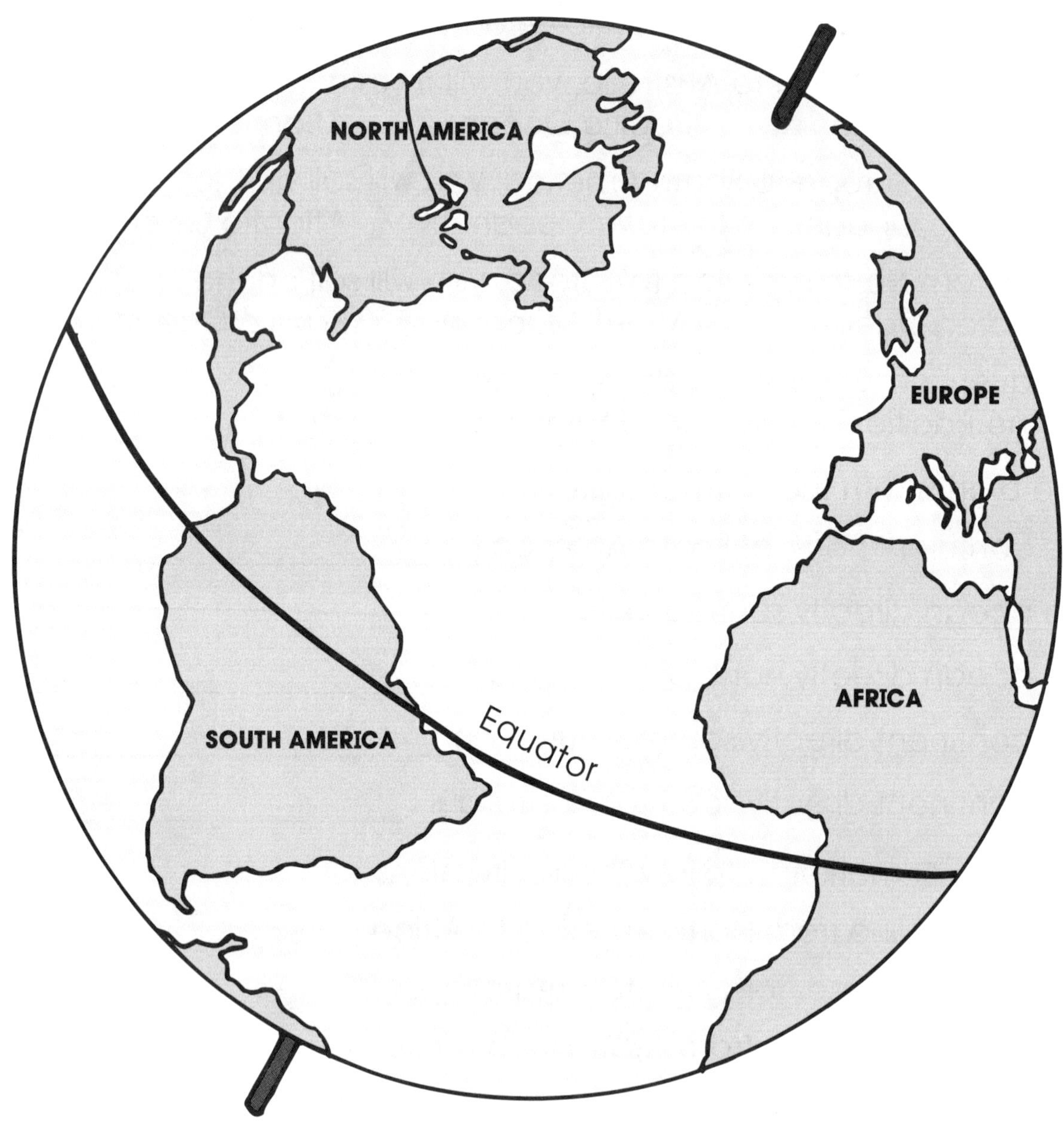

Trace the equator in orange.

Label the two hemispheres on the globe above.

Hemispheres

When the earth is cut in half vertically along an imaginary line called the **prime meridian**, the **Eastern** and **Western Hemispheres** of the earth are created.

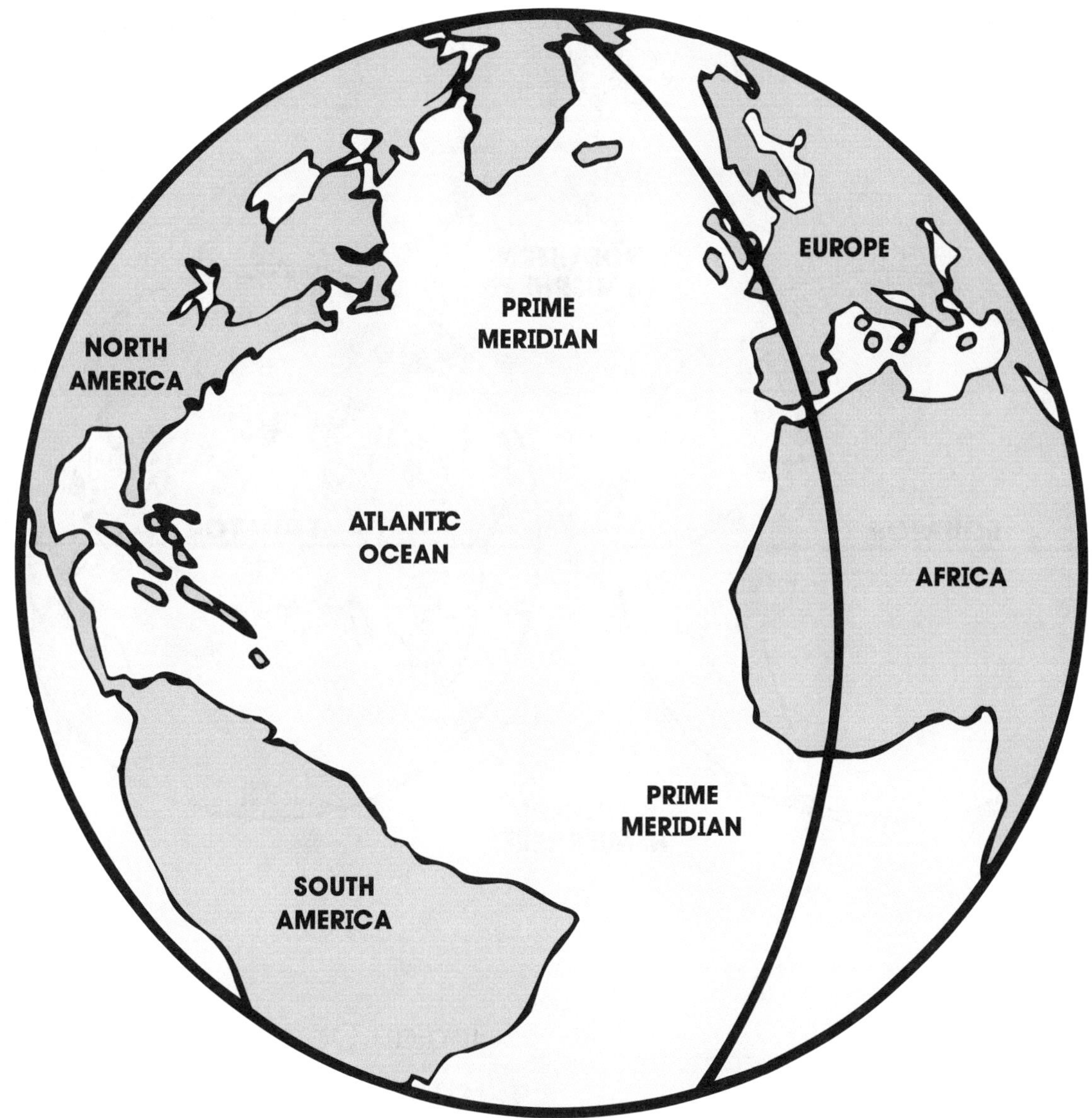

Trace the prime meridian in blue.

Label the two hemispheres on the globe above.

Color the axis, or poles, red.

Hemispheres

Directions: Examine the illustration below. Decide in which two hemispheres (Eastern or Western and Northern or Southern) each of the following continents or oceans is located. (Example: The United States is in the Northern and Western Hemispheres.) Write your answers in the space provided.

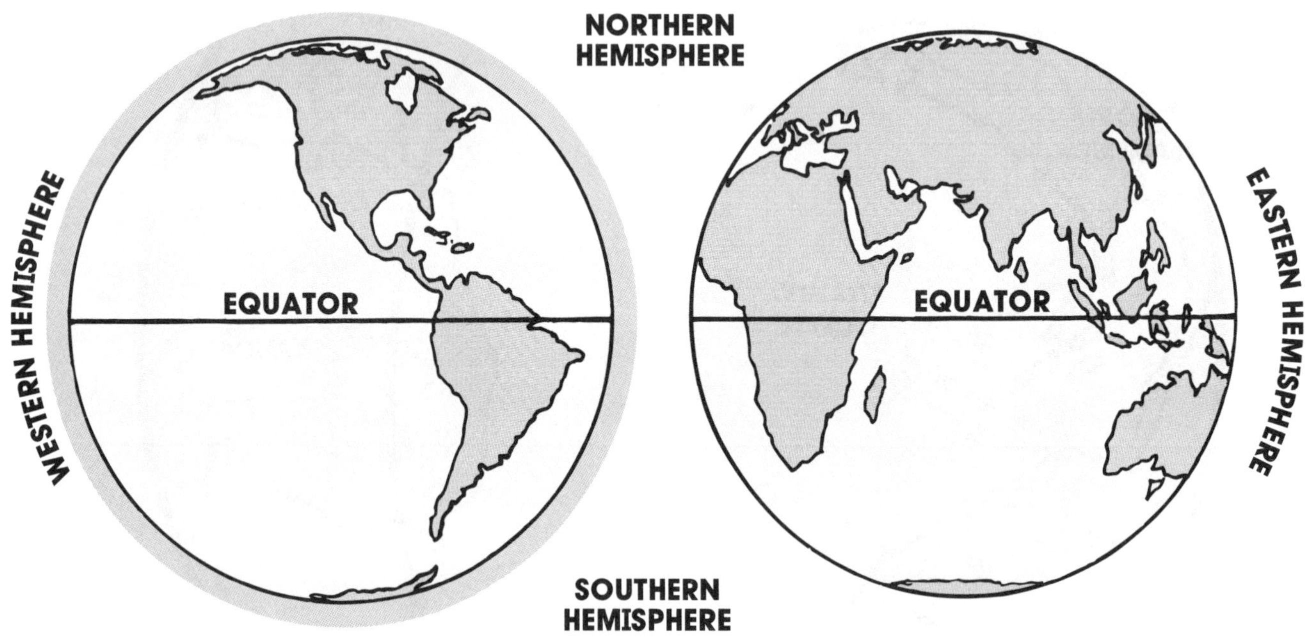

1. North America ______________
2. Europe ______________
3. South America ______________
4. Pacific Ocean ______________
5. Australia ______________
6. Atlantic Ocean ______________
7. Indian Ocean ______________
8. Asia ______________
9. Africa ______________
10. Antarctica ______________
11. Arctic Ocean ______________

Locating the Continents and Oceans

Directions: Use these maps plus wall maps to complete this page. **Note:** Some continents belong to more than one hemisphere.

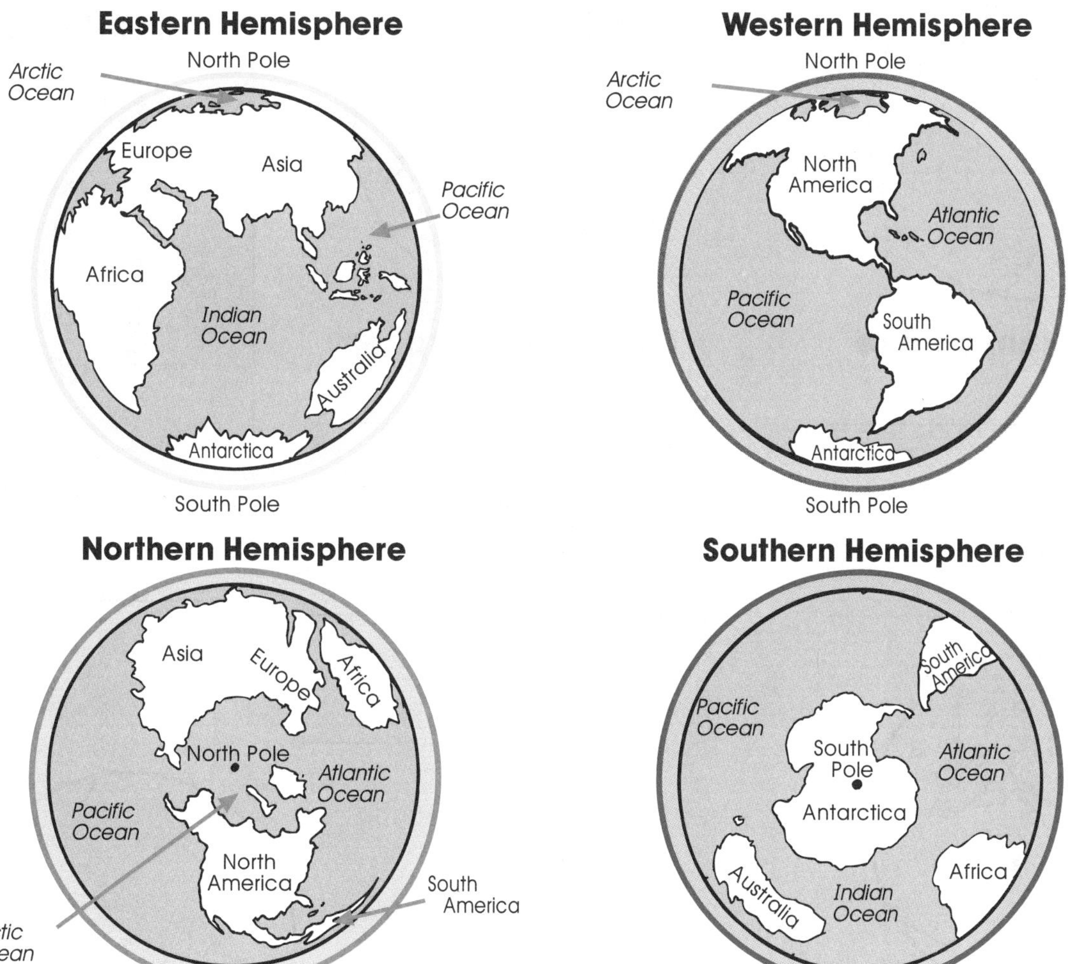

1. Which continent is found in both the Eastern and Western Hemispheres?

____

2. Which map does not show any part of Antarctica?

____

3. Which hemisphere does not include any part of Africa?

____

4. Color the continent located entirely in the Western and Northern Hemispheres red.
5. Color the continent located entirely in the Eastern and Southern Hemispheres green.

Happy Hemispheres

Write the name of each continent and ocean next to its number.

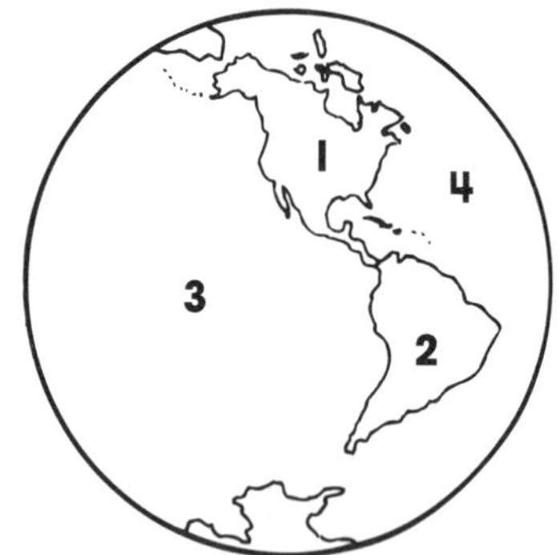

Word Bank

Atlantic
Pacific
Indian
Arctic
North America
South America
Europe
Australia
Asia
Africa
Antarctica

Western Hemisphere

1. ____________________
2. ____________________
3. ____________________
4. ____________________

Eastern Hemisphere

1. ____________________
2. ____________________
3. ____________________
4. ____________________
5. ____________________
6. ____________________

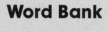

Northern Hemisphere

1. ____________________
2. ____________________
3. ____________________
4. ____________________
5. ____________________
6. ____________________

Southern Hemisphere

1. ____________________
2. ____________________
3. ____________________
4. ____________________
5. ____________________
6. ____________________
7. ____________________

North to South

South Pole

North Pole

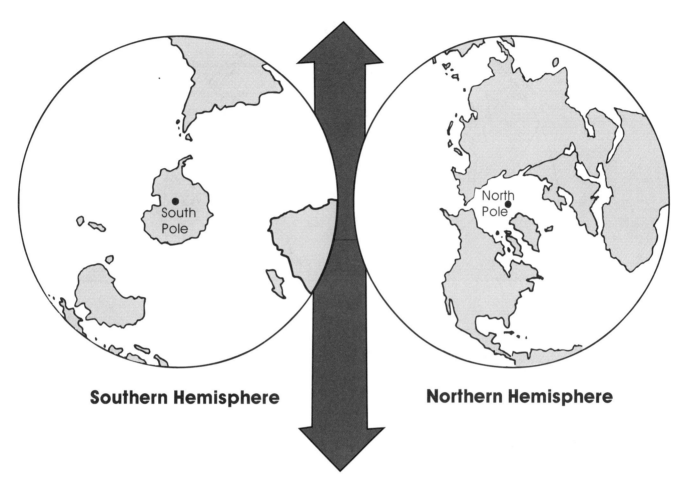

Southern Hemisphere

Northern Hemisphere

Directions: Label the continents on each hemisphere. Use the abbreviations below.

N.A.	=	North America	**Ant.**	=	Antarctica
S.A.	=	South America	**Aust.**	=	Australia
Eur.	=	Europe	**Afr.**	=	Africa
As.	=	Asia			

Color the oceans in each hemisphere using the colors and designs below.

(purple)  Indian Ocean

(green) 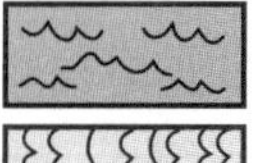 Atlantic Ocean

(blue) 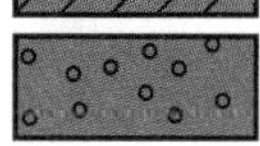 Pacific Ocean

(lt. green) Arctic Ocean

Global Fun

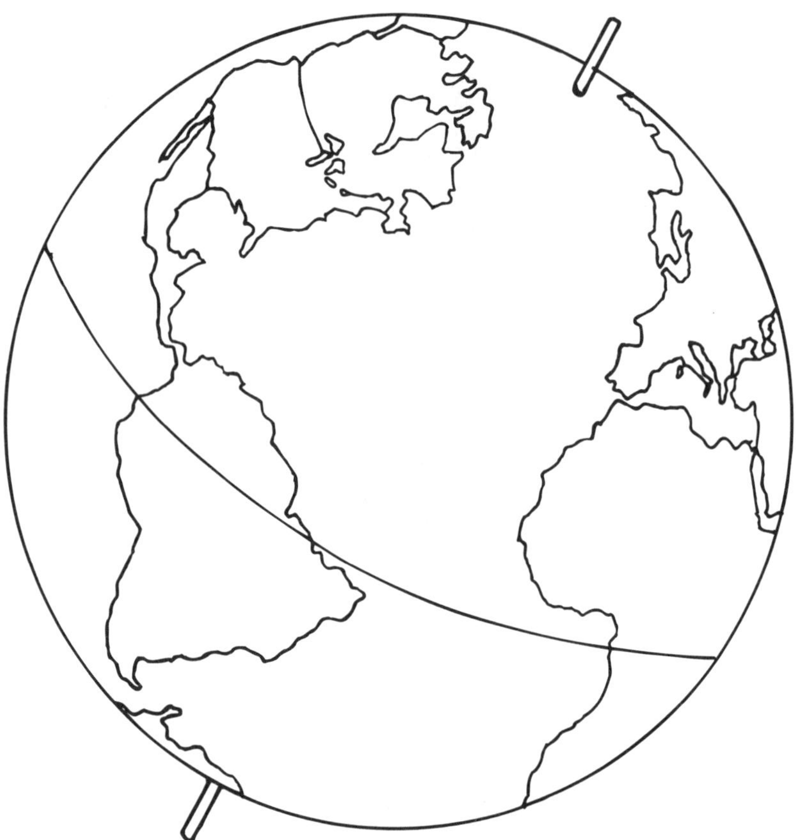

Directions: Complete the globe by following the directions below.

1. Draw a whale in the Southern Hemisphere of the Pacific Ocean.
2. Trace the equator in orange.
3. Draw a shark in the Arctic Ocean.
4. Draw a smiling face near Antarctica.
5. Draw an ocean liner in the Northern Hemisphere of the Atlantic Ocean.
6. Color the axis poles red.
7. In North America, color Mexico yellow, Canada green and the U.S.A. red.
8. Draw a yellow **X** in the Northern Hemisphere of Africa.
9. Color Europe purple.
10. Draw rainbow-colored diagonal stripes on South America.
11. Draw an orange circle on the Southern Hemisphere of Africa.

From East to West

Directions: Label the continents using the abbreviations below. Cut out the continents. Glue them onto the correct hemisphere in the proper places. Include Antarctica on each hemisphere.

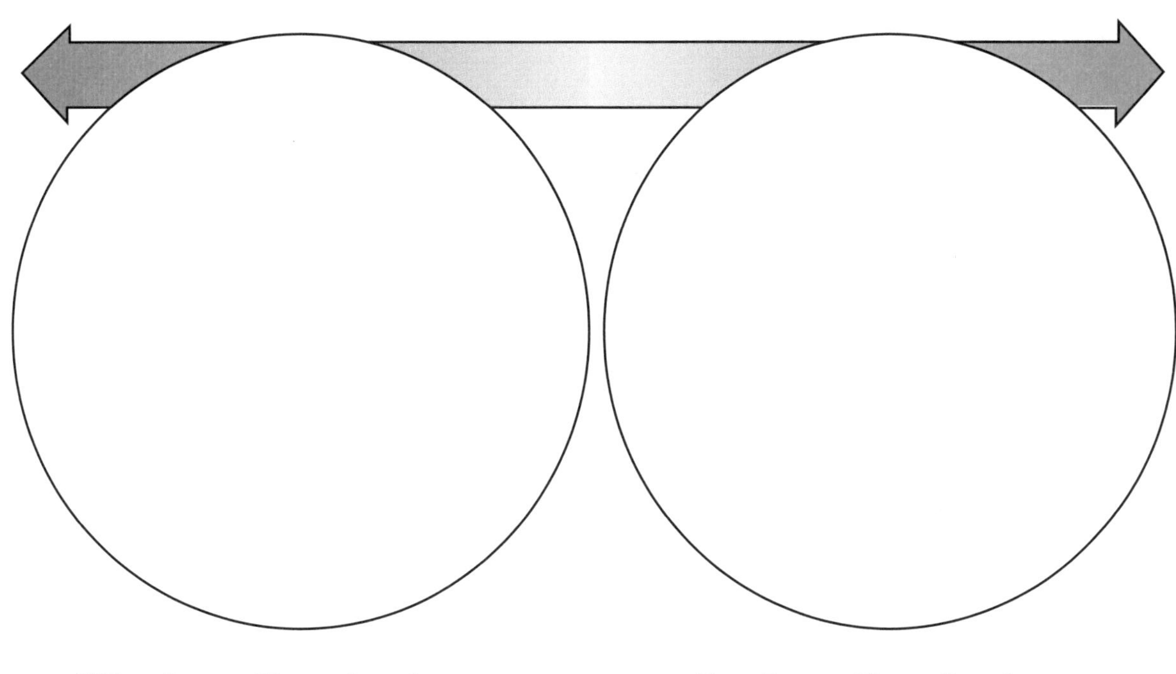

Western Hemisphere **Eastern Hemisphere**

Abbreviations

N.A. = North America
Eur. = Europe
Aust. = Australia
S.A. = South America
As. = Asia
Afr. = Africa
Ant. = Antarctica

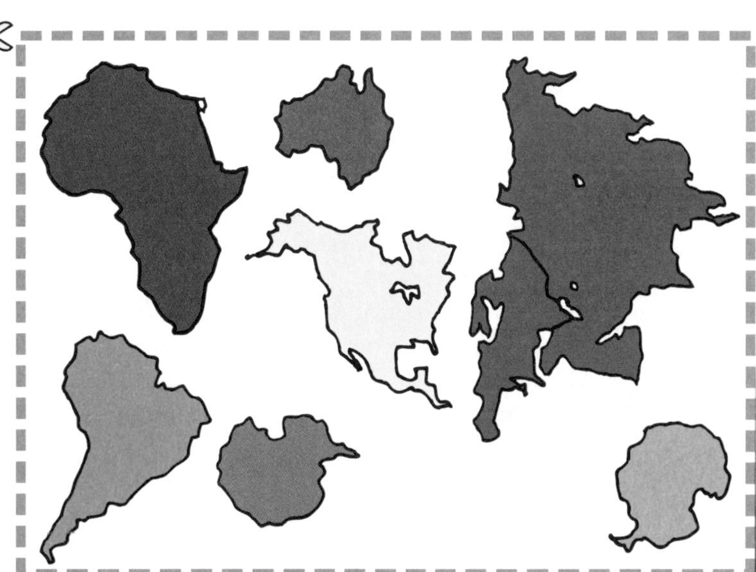

Page is blank for cutting exercise on previous page.

The Long Lines

Lines of longitude on a globe run north and south. They are sometimes called **meridians.** Zero degrees longitude (0°) is an imaginary line called the **prime meridian.** It passes through Greenwich, England. Half of the lines of longitude are west of the prime meridian, and half are east of it.

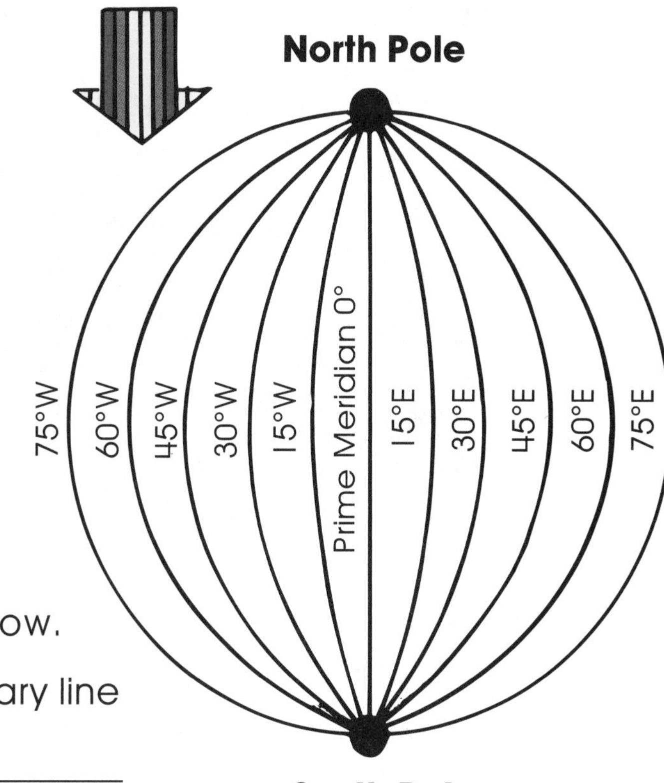

Directions: Answer the questions below.

1. What is the name for the imaginary line at 0° longitude? ____________________
2. Lines to the left of the prime meridian are which direction? ____________________
3. Lines to the right of the prime meridian are which direction? __________
4. Where do lines of longitude come together?
   ______________________ and ________________________
5. Where does the prime meridian pass through?
   ____
6. Lines of longitude run in which directions?
   ______________________ and ________________________
7. Color the prime meridian red.
8. Color the other meridians blue.

Merry Meridians

Shown on the map are the lines of longitude west of the prime meridian.

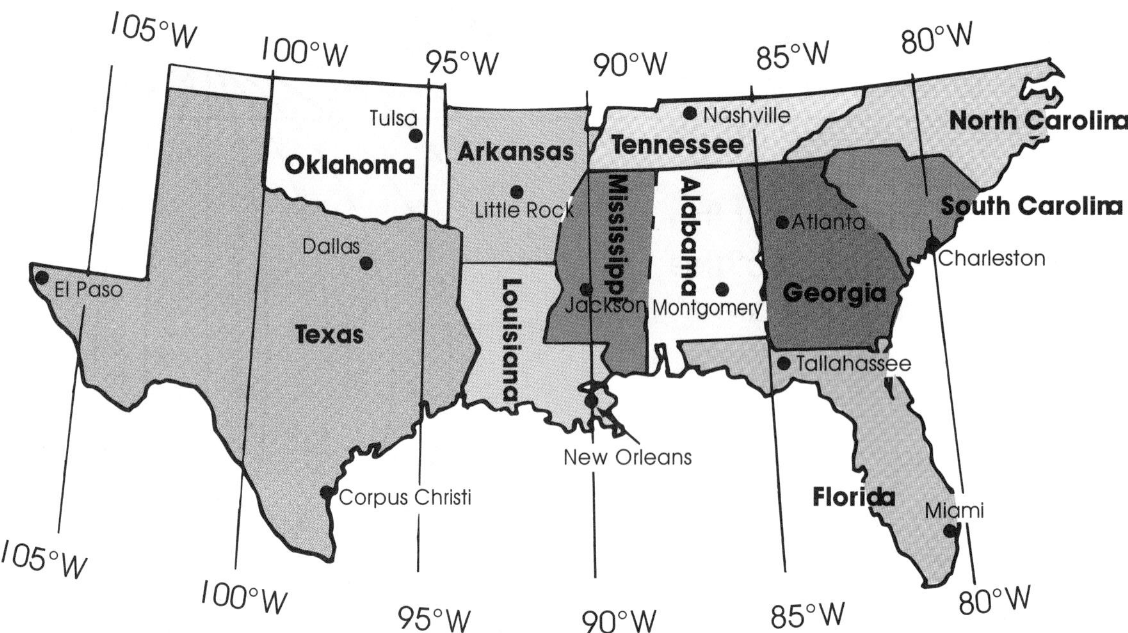

Directions: Answer the questions about these southeastern states.

1. Which two cities lie closest to 90°W?
   ____________________, ______________________,
2. To which longitude line is Miami, Florida, closest? ______________________
3. Which cities lie between 80°W and 85°W? ____________________,
   ____________________, ______________________, ____________________,
4. Which city is closest to 95°W? ______________________________
5. El Paso, Texas, is closest to which meridian? ______________________
6. Which two cities are closest to 85°W? ______________, ______________
7. Little Rock is between which two meridians? ______________ and
   ____
8. Parts of which states lie between 85°W and 90°W? ______________,
   ____________________, ______________________, ____________________,
   ____________________, ______________________, ____________________,
9. Most of Florida lies between which meridians? ______________________
10. Corpus Christi lies between which meridians? ______________________
    and ______________________________

Where Is the Prime Meridian?

Meridians of longitude help people locate places east and west of the prime meridian and are measured in units called degrees (°).

Directions: Complete this page and page 34.

1. What do the letters N, S, E and W stand for?

____

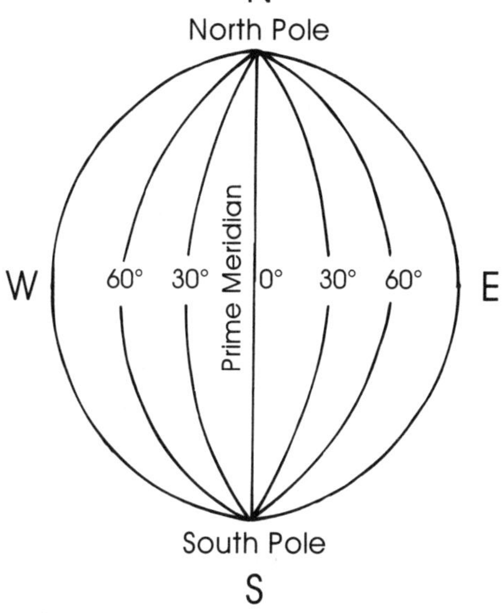

2. The ______________________ is 0° longitude.

3. Meridians of longitude are measured _________________ and _________________ of the prime meridian.

4. Where do all the meridians meet?________

5. Meridians of longitude are measured in units called

____.

Do the following to complete this map.

Hint: The map above will help you.

A. Label the four cardinal directions.

B. Draw a meridian at 30°E and 30°W.

C. Draw a meridian at 60°E and 60°W.

D. Label the North and South Poles.

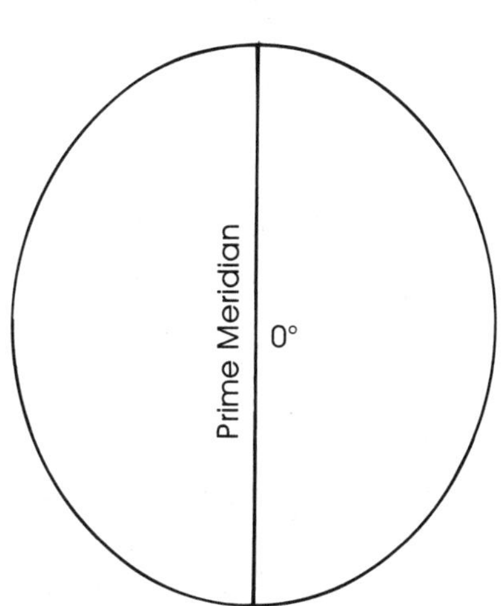

Where Is the Prime Meridian?

Use with page 33.

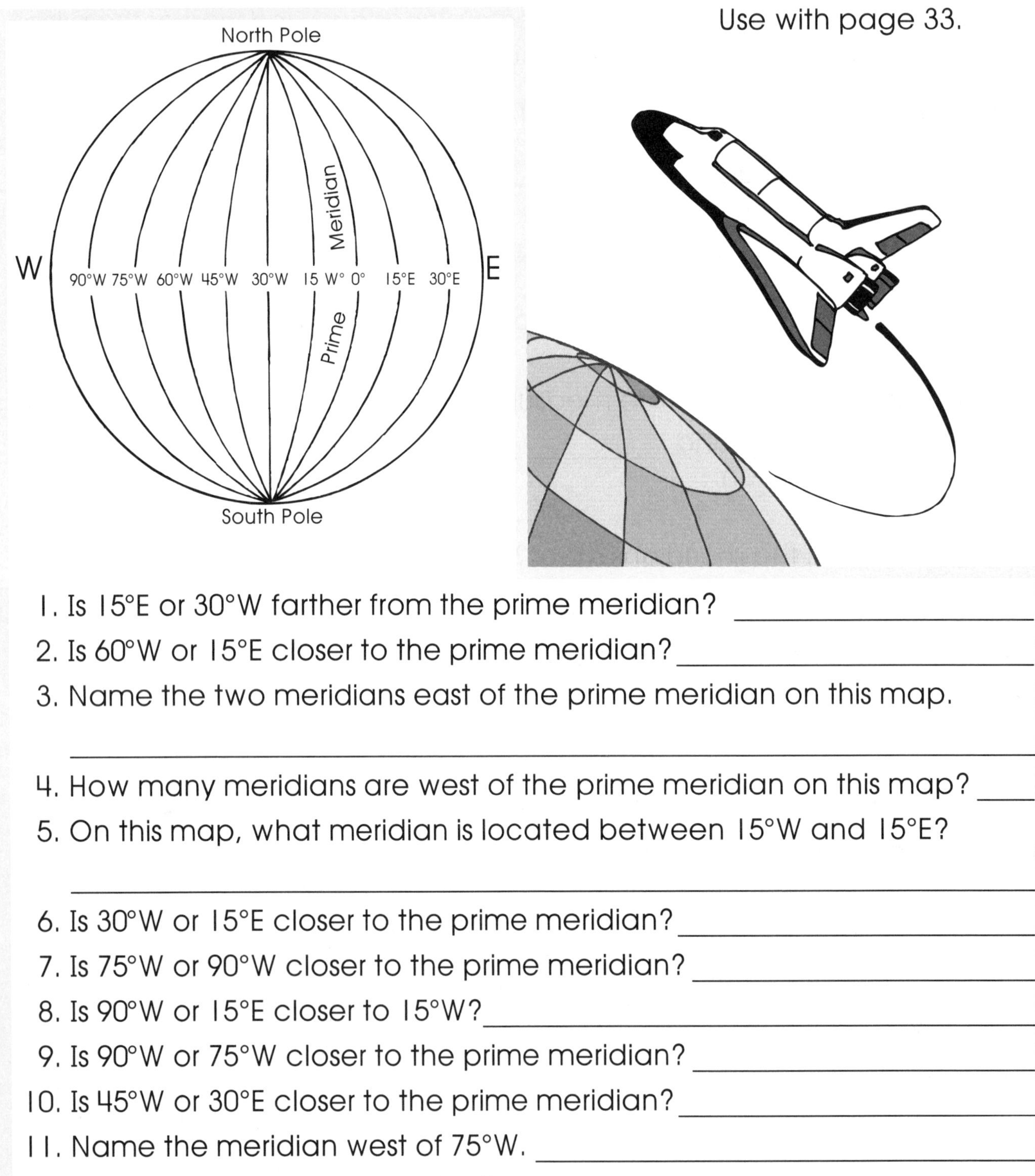

1. Is 15°E or 30°W farther from the prime meridian? ________________

2. Is 60°W or 15°E closer to the prime meridian? ________________

3. Name the two meridians east of the prime meridian on this map.

____

4. How many meridians are west of the prime meridian on this map? ____

5. On this map, what meridian is located between 15°W and 15°E?

____

6. Is 30°W or 15°E closer to the prime meridian? ________________

7. Is 75°W or 90°W closer to the prime meridian? ________________

8. Is 90°W or 15°E closer to 15°W? ________________

9. Is 90°W or 75°W closer to the prime meridian? ________________

10. Is 45°W or 30°E closer to the prime meridian? ________________

11. Name the meridian west of 75°W. ________________

12. Name the meridian east of 15°E. ________________

Lines of Longitude

Directions: Use the meridians shown in the globe below to answer the questions.

1. Lines of longitude are called
   ______________________________.
2. They run in which directions?
   ___________and ____________
3. 0° longitude passes through
   ______________________________.
4. 0° longitude is called the
   ______________________________.
5. Degrees to the right of the prime meridian are which direction?

6. What meridian is west of 75°W? ____________________________________

7. Degrees to the left of the prime meridian are which direction? _______
8. Name the meridians east of 0° on this globe. __________ ____________
9. What meridian is east of 15°W? _____________
10. Which meridians shown on this map pass through the continent of Africa?__________________________________
11. What meridian is west of 45°W? ______________
12. Trace the prime meridian orange.
13. Trace the other meridians yellow.

Locating Cities

This map shows part of the northeastern United States. All longitude meridians on this map are west.

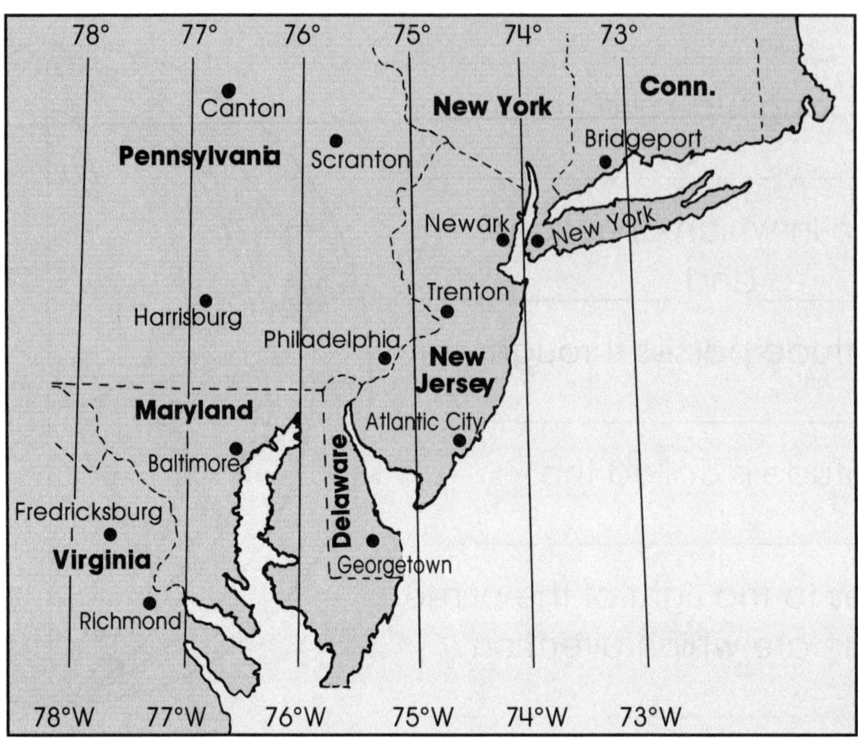

Directions: Use the longitude meridians above to answer the questions below.

1. Bridgeport, Connecticut, is closest to which meridian? ______________
2. Trenton, New Jersey is closest to which meridian? ___________________
3. Name the meridians closest to these cities:

   Philadelphia _________ Georgetown __________

   Scranton _________ Newark ____________
4. Name the seven states shown on this map. ____________________

   __________________ ___________________ ______________________

   __________________ ___________________ ______________________
5. Atlantic City is between ___________ and _________ longitude.
6. Harrisburg is closest to which meridian? ______________________
7. Which is farther west—Harrisburg or Philadelphia? ___________________
8. Richmond is closest to __________________longitude.

North and South Dakota

Directions: Use this map to answer the questions. All longitude meridians will be west.

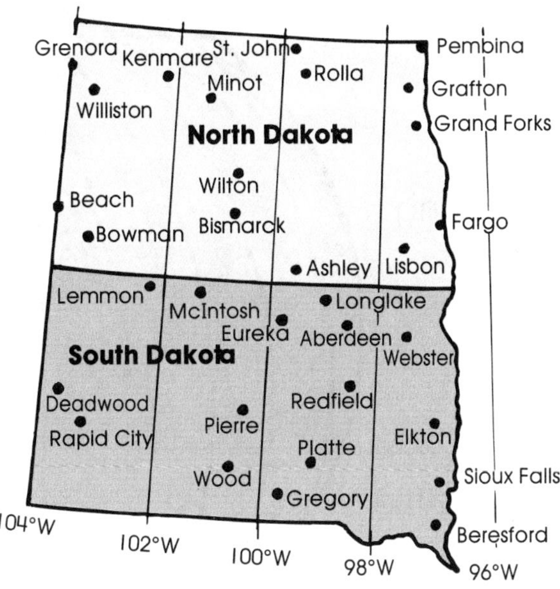

1. Which meridian is closest to Eureka, South Dakota? ________________
2. Which town is closer to 98°W—Platte, South Dakota or Lisbon, North Dakota? ________________________________
3. Grenora, North Dakota is located almost exactly on the ______ meridian.
4. Is Deadwood, South Dakota north or south of Rapid City? ____________
5. Which town is closer to 104°W—Bowman, North Dakota or Lemmon, South Dakota? ________________________________
6. If you were traveling east from Rapid City, which meridian would you arrive at first? __________
7. Which meridian would you reach first when traveling east from Sioux Falls, South Dakota? ________________
8. Bismarck is in the state of ______________________.
9. Lemmon, South Dakota is closest to the ____________ meridian.
10. Name the North Dakota cities located east of 98°W longitude.

____

____

____

Lines of Longitude

Remember... The lines of longitude tell how far east or west of the **prime meridian** (0°) you are.

All lines of longitude are measured from the prime meridian in degrees. Everything west of the prime meridian is labeled **W** for **west**, and everything east of the prime meridian is labeled **E** for **east**.

Directions: Use a globe or map to find the longitude for each of the following cities. Remember to indicate both the number of degrees and whether it is east or west of the prime meridian.

NORTH POLE

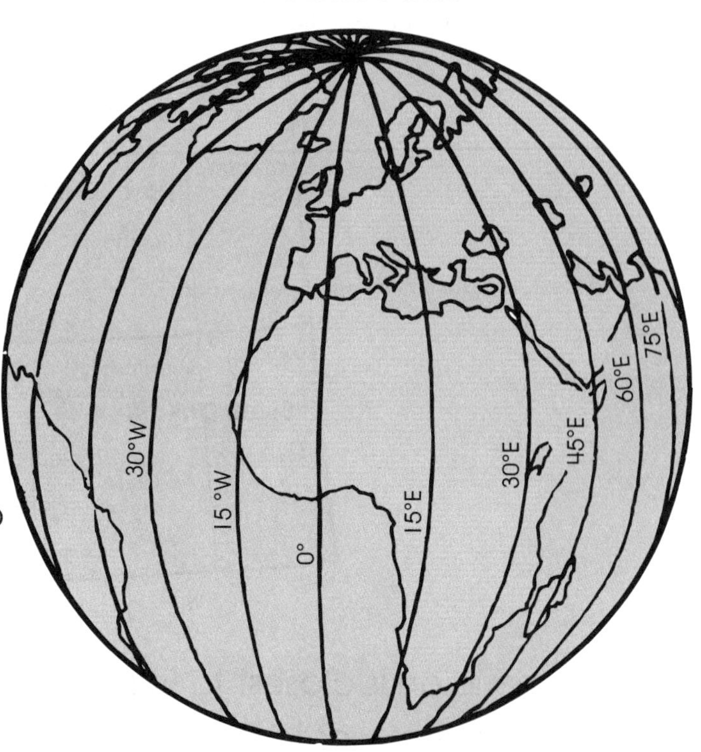

SOUTH POLE

1. Los Angeles, U.S.A. ________________
2. London, England ________________
3. Wellington, New Zealand ________________
4. Tokyo, Japan ________________
5. Bangkok, Thailand ________________
6. Santiago, Chile ________________
7. Nairobi, Kenya ________________
8. Tehran, Iran ________________
9. Paris, France ________________
10. Glasgow, Scotland ________________
11. Rome, Italy ________________
12. Buenos Aires, Argentina ________________
13. Anchorage, Alaska ________________
14. Calcutta, India ________________
15. Cairo, Egypt ________________
16. Shanghai, China ________________

Locating Cities in Europe

Directions: Use this map to answer the questions. Pay particular attention to the location of the prime meridian.

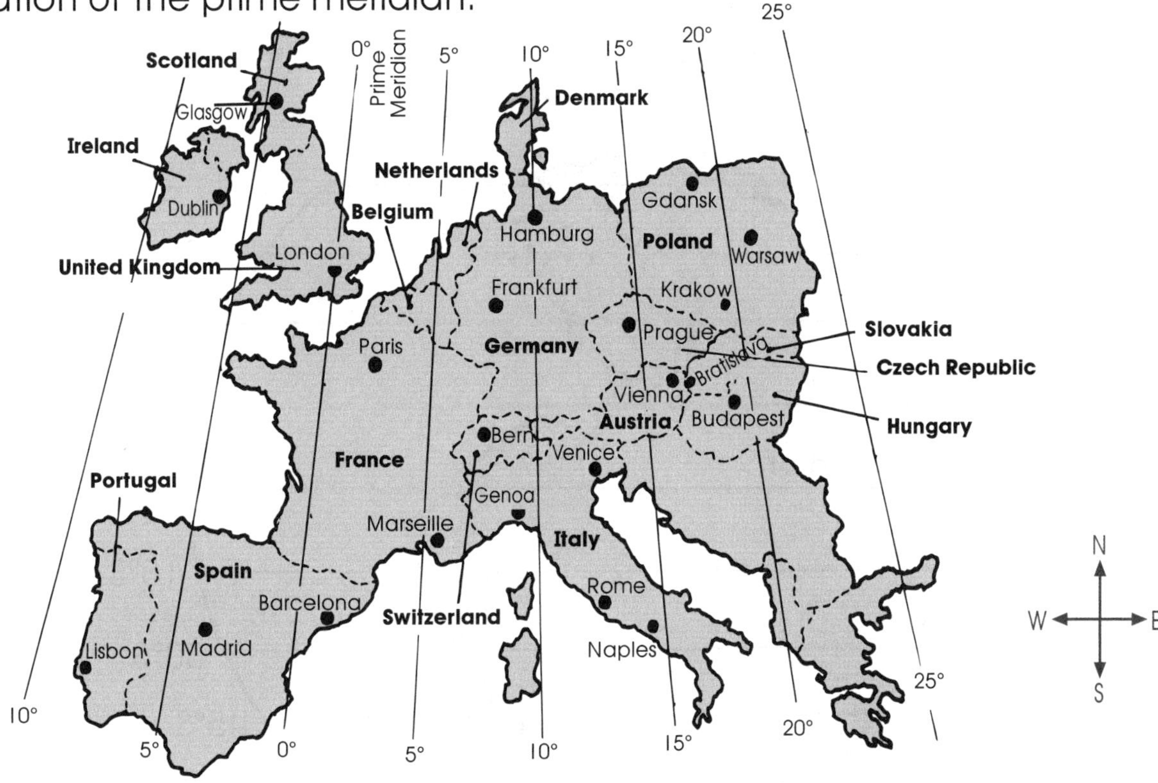

1. On the map label each longitude meridian either east or west.
2. Rome, Italy, is located between the __________ and __________ meridians.
3. Which meridian passes through the western edge of Ireland? ______________
4. Portugal is located between the __________ and __________ meridians.
5. Between which two meridians is Switzerland located? ______________
6. Explain how you would decide which of the 5° meridians is east and which is west. ______________________________
7. Warsaw is closest to the ____________________ meridian.
8. Marseille, France, is which direction from the 5°E meridian? ______________
9. Gdansk is in the country of ____________________.
10. Prague is __________________ of 15°E longitude.
11. Hamburg is on the ____________________ meridian.
12. Marseille is almost on the ____________________ meridian of longitude.

Lines of Latitude

Lines of latitude on a globe are called parallels. They run east and west. The equator is at 0° latitude. Use the map below to answer the questions.

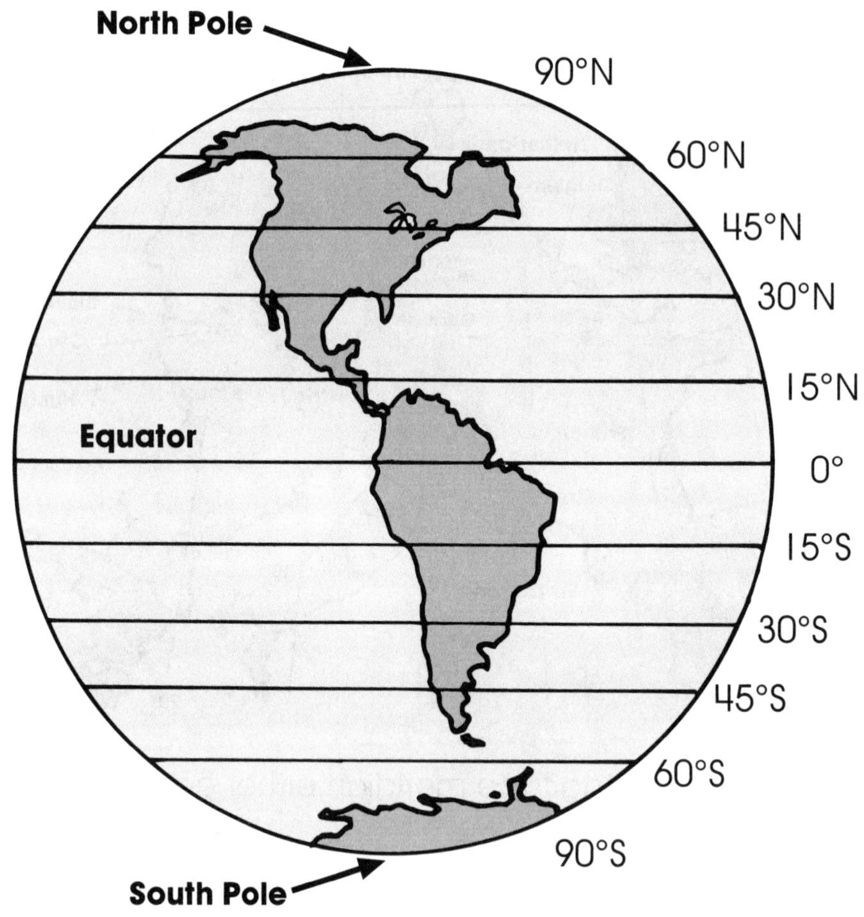

1. 0° latitude is called the ____________________.
2. Lines of latitude are called ____________________.
3. Parallels run which directions? ____________ and ____________
4. The latitude of the North Pole is ____________________.
5. Which parallel runs through Florida? ____________________
6. What is located at 90°S latitude? ____________________
7. Which parallel runs through Canada? ____________________
8. Lines of latitude above the equator are which direction? ____________
9. Below the equator, the parallels are which direction? ____________

Lateral Movement

Parallels measure the distance north or south from the equator. Zero degrees latitude (0°) is at the equator. Half of the parallels are north of the equator and half are south of it. The lines do not meet.

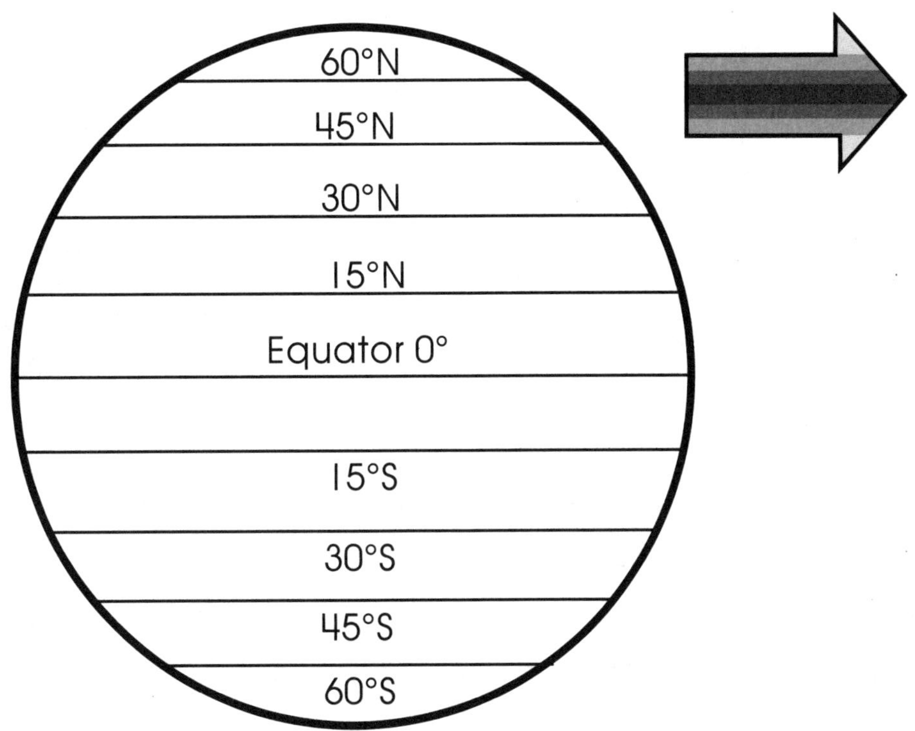

1. What is the symbol for degrees? ____________
2. Latitude lines run ____________ and ____________.
3. Latitude lines are called ________________.
4. Give the latitude of the equator. ________________
5. The parallels above the equator are which direction? ______________
6. The parallels below the equator are which direction? ______________
7. Color the equator parallel orange.
8. Color 15°N and 15°S green.
9. Color 30°N and 30°S blue.
10. Color 45°N and 45°S red.
11. Color 60°N and 60°S purple.

Imaginary Lines

Directions: Answer the questions below using these maps.

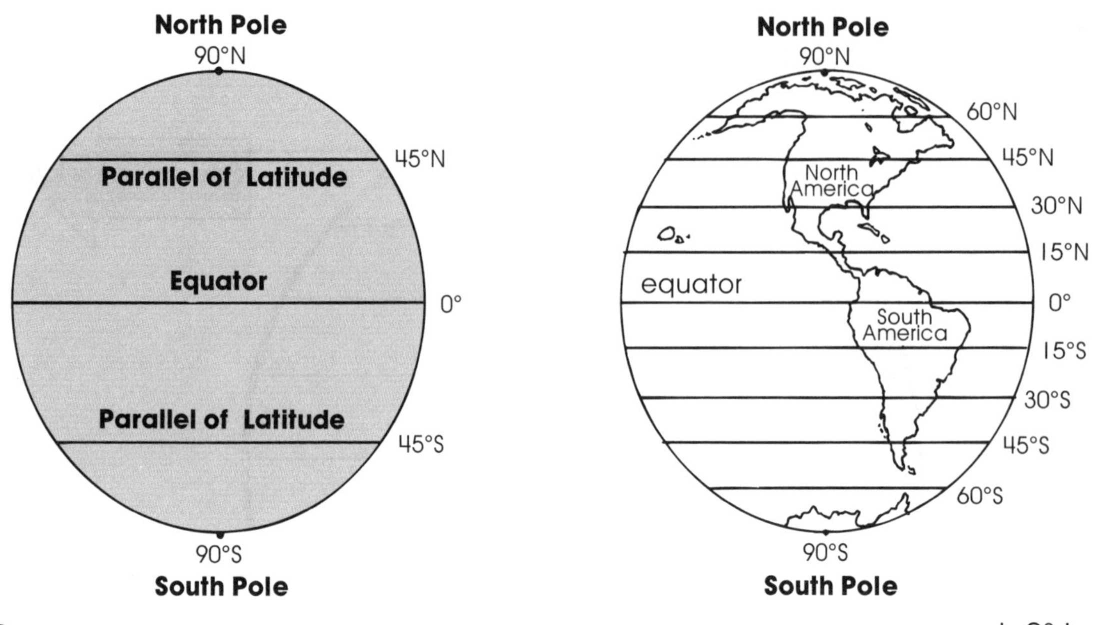

1. The ________________________________ is 0° latitude.
2. The North Pole is ________________________ degrees north latitude.
4. Lines north and south of the equator are called ______________________.
5. The ________________________________ is 90°S latitude.
6. Which line is closer to the equator—30°N or 15°S? ______________________
7. Which is closer to the South Pole—45°S or 30°S? ______________________
8. At what degree is the South Pole? ______________________________
9. If you wanted to find a city located at 45°N, would you look above or below the equator? ____________________
10. Which continent on the map is entirely north of the equator? ________________
11. South America lies between the parallels of latitude ________________°N and 60°S.
12. The equator runs through the northern part of the continent of ________________.
13. Color all the land north of the equator red.
14. Color all of the land south of the equator green.

What's My Line?

There are several important lines of latitude on the globe which have special names.

Directions: Use a map, globe or other resource to identify the special lines on the illustration of the globe below.

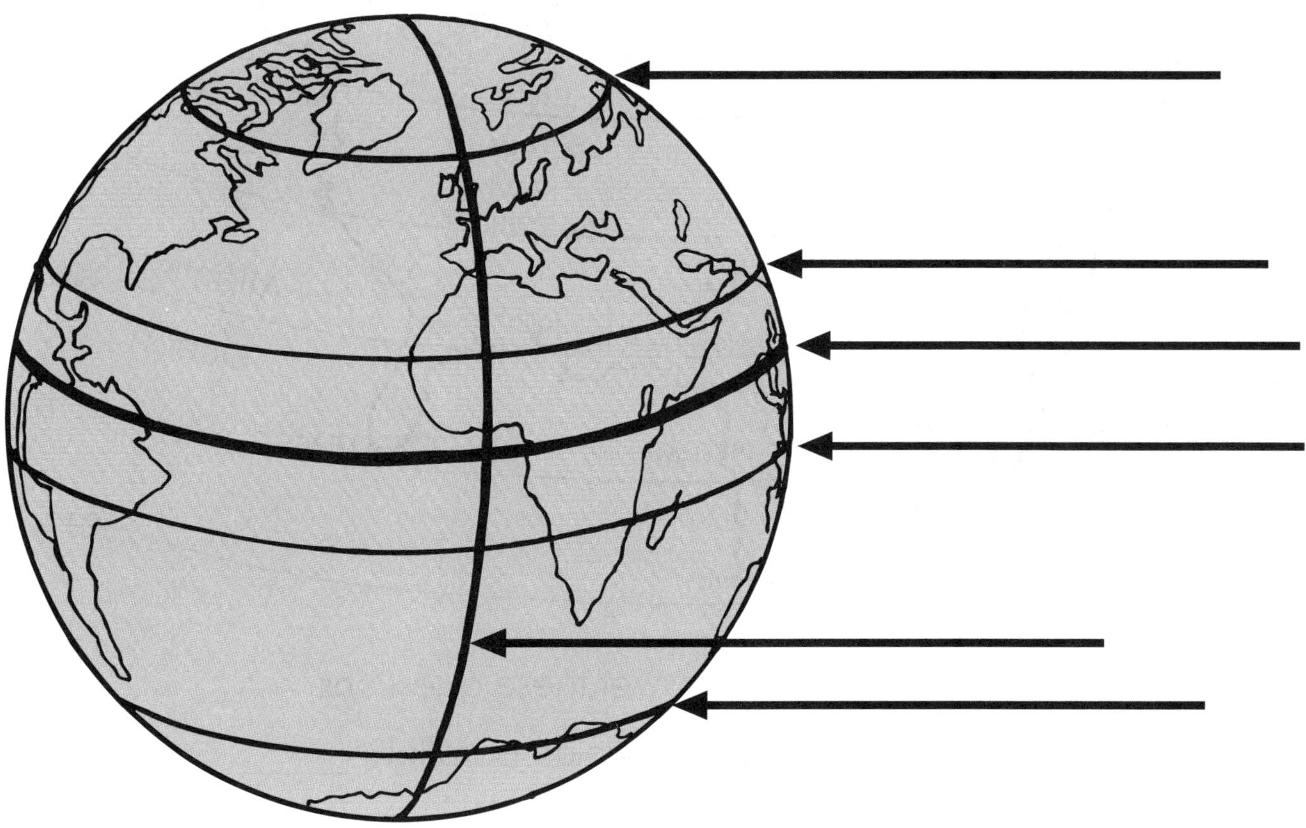

Name the imaginary line that . . .

passes through Mexico. ______________________

is 0° latitude. ______________________

passes through Alaska. ______________________

is 0° longitude. ______________________

divides the Northern and Southern hemispheres. ________________

passes through Botswana. ______________________

Across the U.S.A.

Directions: Use the map above to answer these questions.

1. Denver and New York are close to which parallel? ________________
2. Which two cities are between 45°N and 50°N? ________________
3. Los Angeles and Memphis are near which parallel? ________________
4. Tallahassee is closest to which parallel? ________________
5. St. Louis is between which parallels? ____________ and ____________
6. Which city is farthest north? ________________ It is between which parallels? ________________ and ____________
7. Which city is farthest south? ________________ It is between which parallels? ________________ and ____________
8. San Francisco is halfway between ____________ and ____________.

Latitude in North America

Use with page 46.

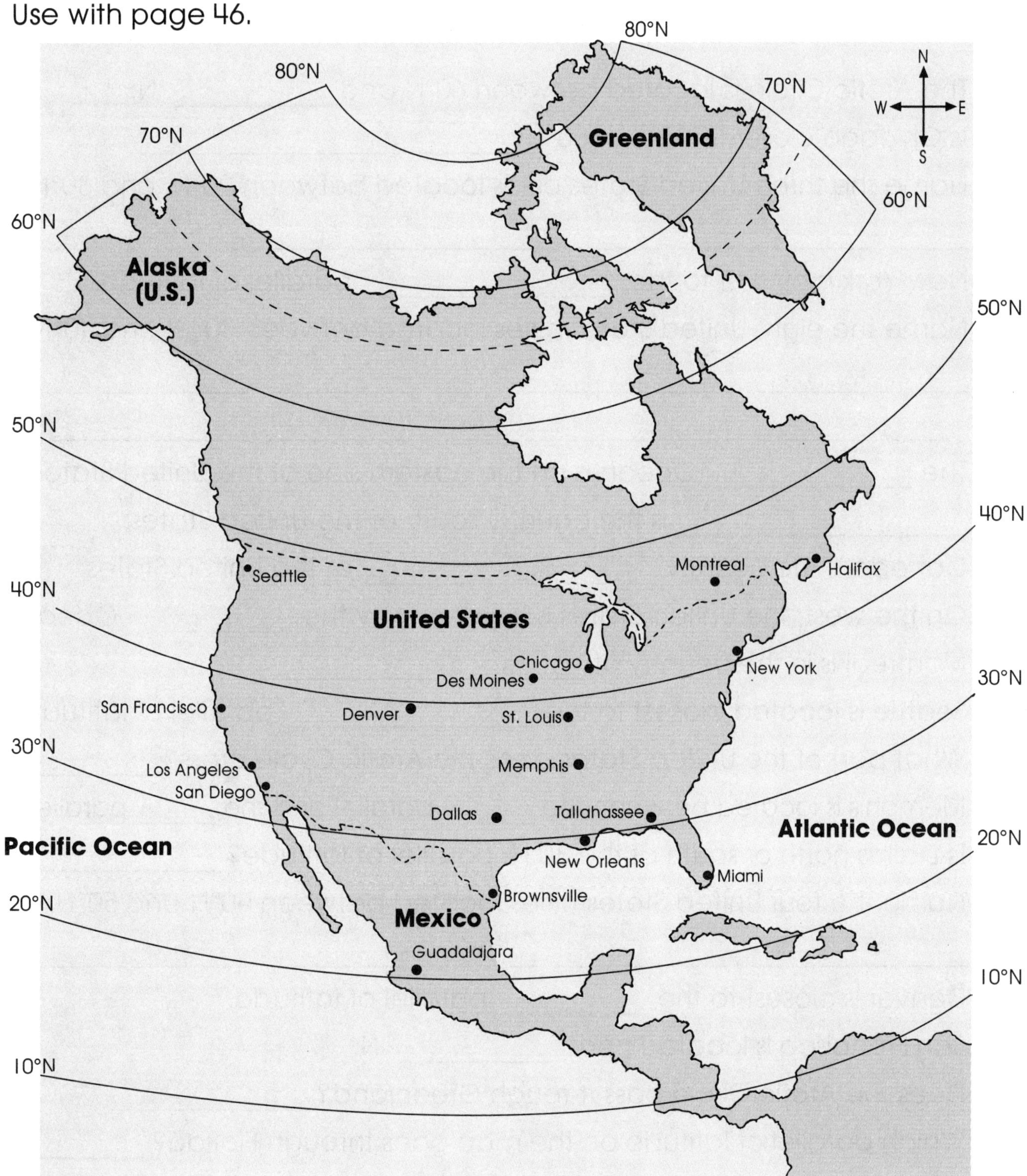

Latitude in North America

Directions: Use the map on page 45 to answer the questions below.

1. The Arctic Circle is located between 60°N and __________ °N.
2. Is Chicago closer to 40°N or 50°N? ________________________
3. Name the three United States cities located between 20°N and 30°N.

   ___________________ ____________________ ____________________

4. New York is closest to the ________________ parallel of latitude.
5. Name the eight United States cities located between 30° N and 40°N.

   ______________ ______________ ______________ ______________

   ______________ ______________ ______________ ______________

6. The _____________ Ocean is on the eastern side of the United States.
7. ___________________ is the country south of the United States.
8. Canada is the country ___________________ of the United States.
9. On the west, the United States is bordered by the ___________ Ocean.
10. Montreal is in the country of _____________________.
11. Seattle is located closest to the ________________ parallel of latitude.
12. What part of the United States does the Arctic Circle cross? __________
13. Memphis is located between the ______ parallel and the ______ parallel.
14. Is Dallas north or south of the 30°N parallel of latitude? _____________
15. Name the four United States cities located between 40°N and 50°N.

    ______________ ______________ ______________ ______________

16. Denver is closest to the __________ parallel of latitude.
17. San Francisco is located near __________ °N.
18. Does the Arctic Circle pass through Greenland? _____________
19. Which parallel of latitude on the map goes through Florida? ________
20. Guadalajara is located in what country? ________________________

Parallels Help With Location

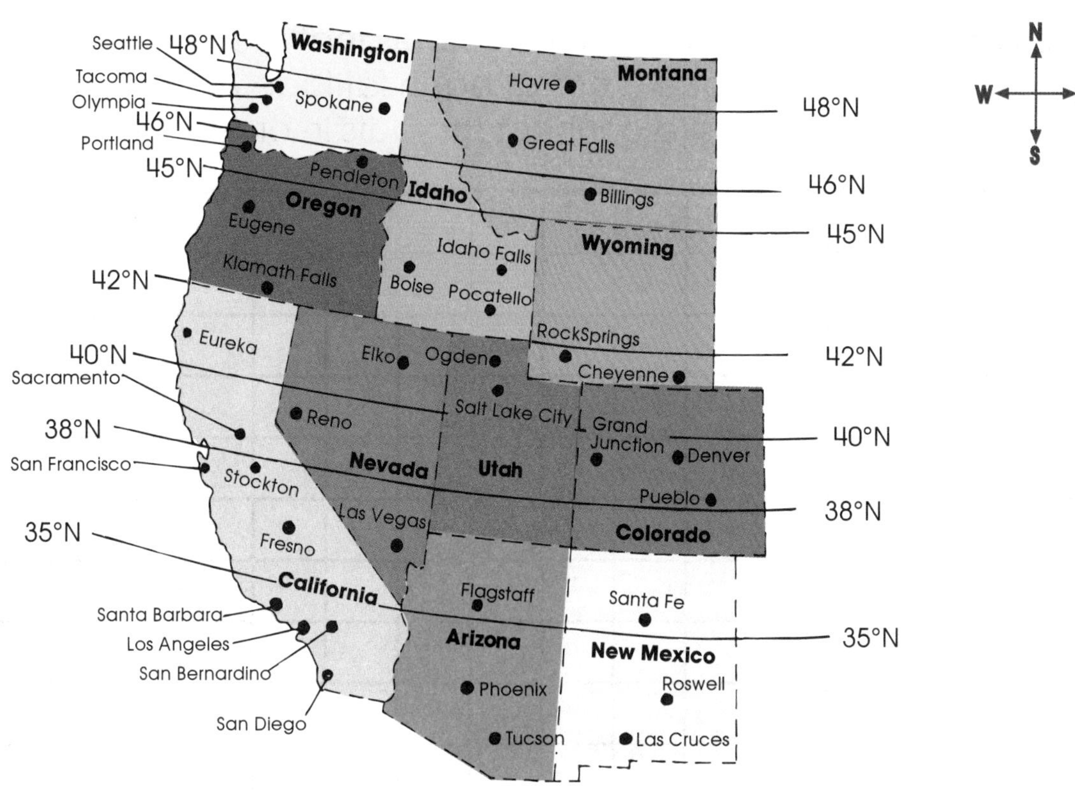

1. Billings, Montana is which direction from the 46°N parallel? ______________
2. Pueblo, Colorado is almost directly on the ____________ parallel of latitude.
3. The boundary between Oregon and California is formed by the ____ parallel.
4. The state of Wyoming is located between 41°N parallel and _______ parallel.
5. Name three cities in Idaho south of the 45°N parallel of latitude.

   ______________________ ______________________ ______________________

6. Which of these cities is south of the 35°N parallel—Flagstaff, Arizona or Roswell, New Mexico? ____
7. Name the three California cities located between the 35°N and 38°N parallels.

   ______________________ ______________________ ______________________

8. All of the cities shown in Washington are between the parallels of ____________ and ____________.
9. Which two Nevada cities are north of the 38°N parallel? ________________ and __________________
10. Klamath Falls, Oregon is almost directly on the ___________ parallel.

Picture It!

Directions: Coordinates are sets of numbers that show where lines of latitude and longitude meet. Place a dot at each latitude / longitude coordinate on the graph. Draw lines to connect the dots in order.

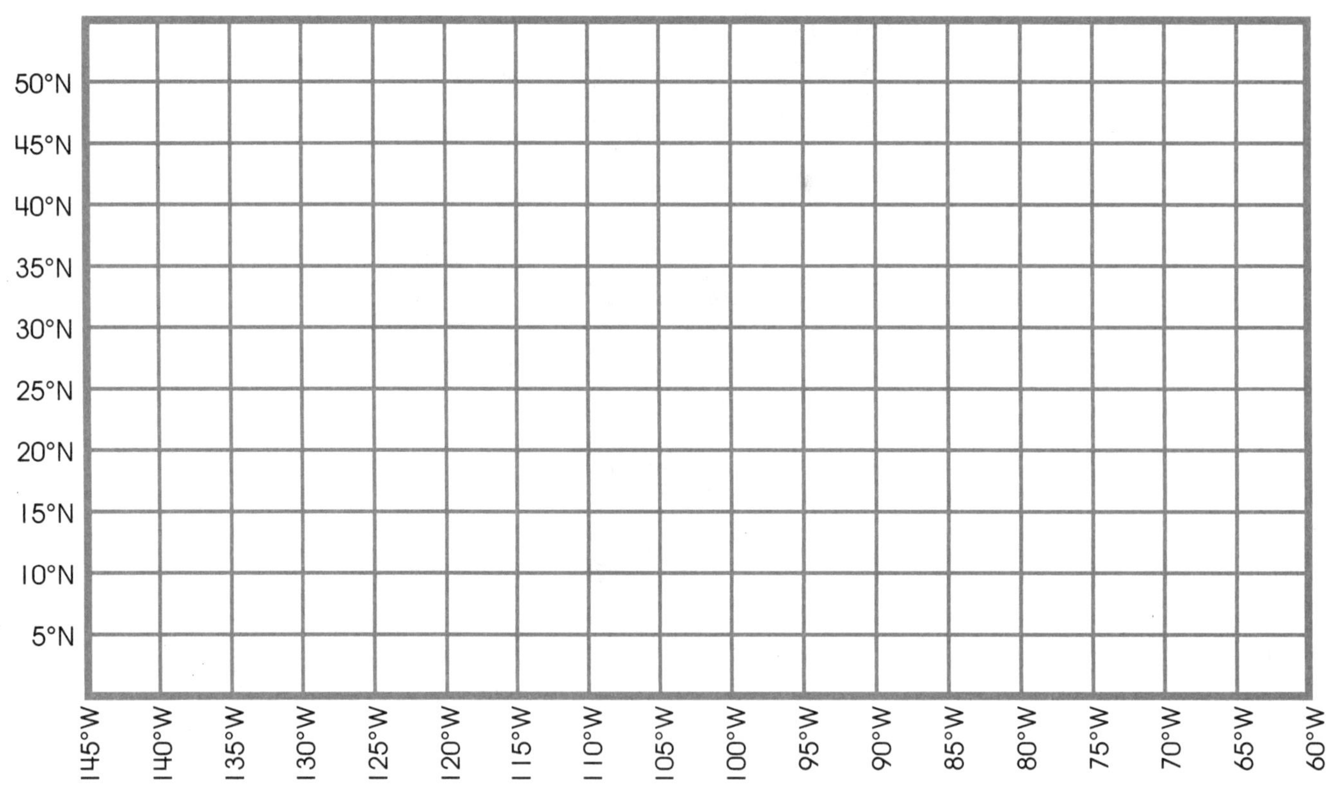

1. 30°N / 140°W
2. 25°N / 135°W
3. 20°N / 130°W
4. 15°N / 125°W
5. 15°N / 90°W
6. 20°N / 85°W
7. 25°N / 80°W
8. 30°N / 75°W
9. 30°N / 90°W
10. 45°N / 90°W
11. 45°N / 100°W
12. 30°N / 100°W
13. 30°N / 110°W
14. 45°N / 110°W
15. 45°N / 120°W
16. 30°N / 120°W
17. 30°N / 140°W

Now place a yellow **X** at each coordinate below. Do not connect the **X**s.

1. 45°N / 140°W
2. 35°N / 135°W
3. 45°N / 130°W
4. 40°N / 80°W
5. 45°N / 70°W
6. 35°N / 65°W

Color the rest of the picture.

What Will They Be?

Directions: Place a dot at each of these latitude and longitude points on the graph.

1. 45°N / 105°W
2. 40°N / 110°W
3. 35°N / 115°W
4. 30°N / 120°W
5. 25°N / 125°W
6. 20°N / 120°N
7. 15°N / 115°W
8. 10°N / 110°W
9. 5°N / 105°W
10. 10°N / 100°W
11. 15°N / 95°W
12. 20°N / 90°W
13. 25°N / 85°W
14. 30°N / 90°W
15. 35°N / 95°W
16. 40°N / 100°W

Draw a line to connect the dots in order. What have you drawn?__________

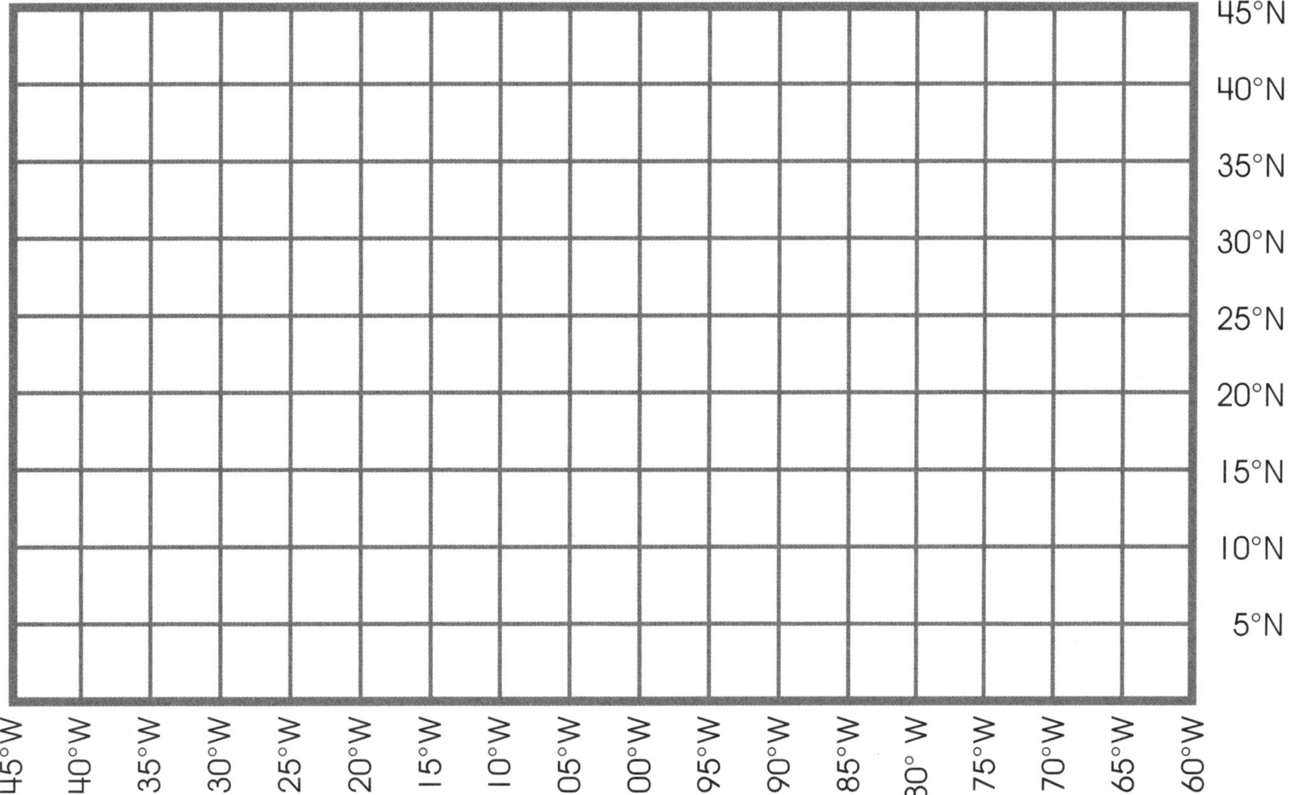

Now with a different color, place a dot at each of these latitude and longitude points.

1. 45°N / 85°W
2. 35°N / 85°W
3. 35°N / 65°W
4. 45°N / 65°W

Connect the dots. What have you drawn? ____________________

Using Lines to Draw a State

Directions: Place a dot on the grid for each point given. The first two have been done for you.

1. 38°N / 99°W	10. 31°N / 104°W	19. 28°N / 97 1/2°W
2. 38° N / 102°W	11. 30°N / 104°W	20. 29°N / 96 1/2°W
3. 36°N / 102°W	12. 29 1/2°N / 103°W	21. 30°N / 95°W
4. 34°N / 102°W	13. 30°N / 102°W	22. 31°N / 94°W
5. 34°N / 104°W	14. 30°N / 101°W	23. 33°N / 94°W
6. 34°N / 106°W	15. 29°N / 101°W	24. 35°N / 94°W
7. 33°N / 105 1/2°W	16. 28°N / 100°W	25. 35°N / 96°W
8. 32 1/2°N / 105°W	17. 27 1/2°N / 99°W	26. 35°N / 99°W
9. 32°N / 104 1/2°W	18. 26 1/2°N / 97 1/2°W	27. 37°N / 99°W

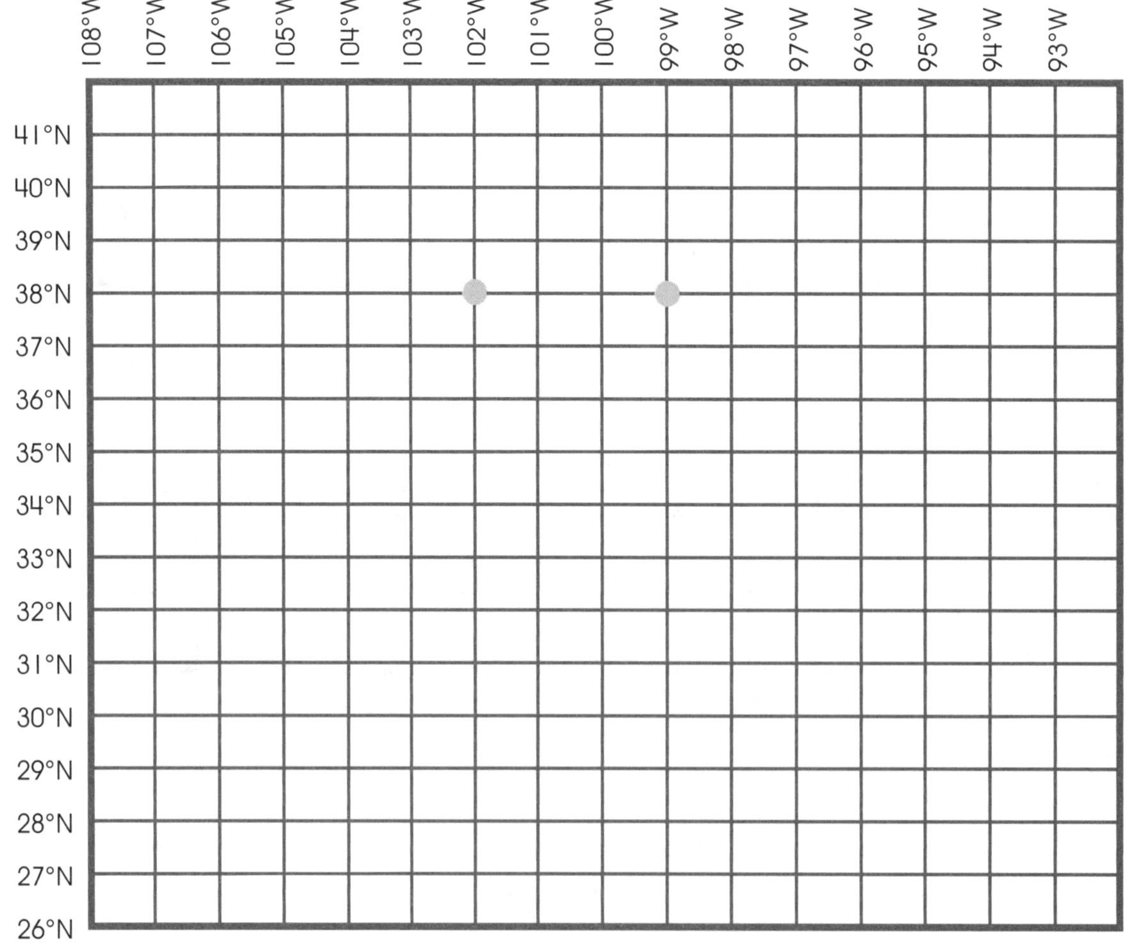

Draw a line to connect all of the dots in order. What state did you draw?

Casey's Island

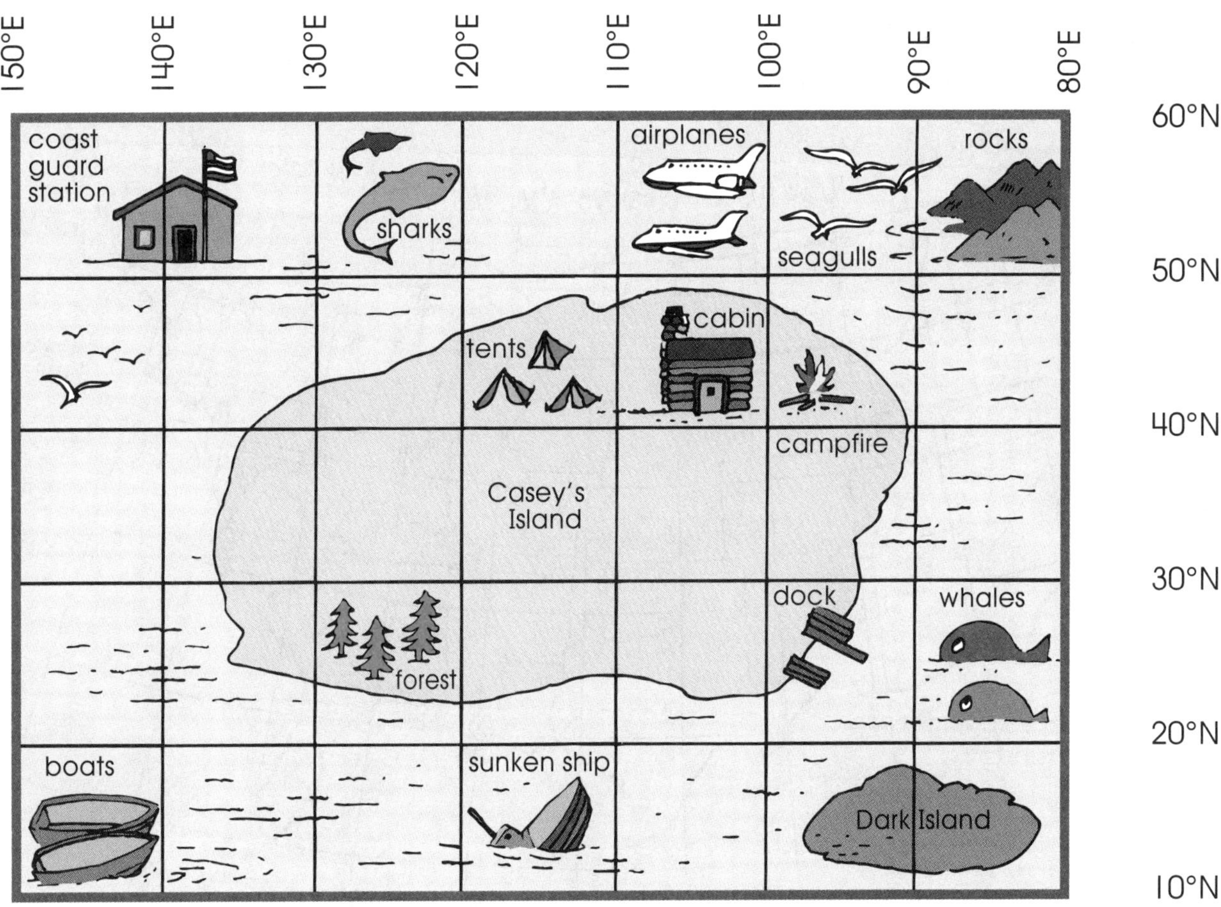

Directions: Use the map above to answer the questions below.

1. The whales are between which two latitude lines? ________________
2. The coast guard station is located between which longitude lines? ______
3. If the whales go north to 55°N latitude, what will they hit? ____________
4. The boats must cross what longitude lines to get to the sunken ship? _____

   ____
5. If you draw a latitude line at 35°N, what will you cross? ____________
6. If the whales cross 90°E longitude, what will they reach? ____________
7. Name the items crossed by the 55°N latitude line. ____________

   ____
8. Which longitude lines cross Casey's Island? ____________

State Search

Which state is roughly between the coordinates given? After locating the state, color it on the map as directed.

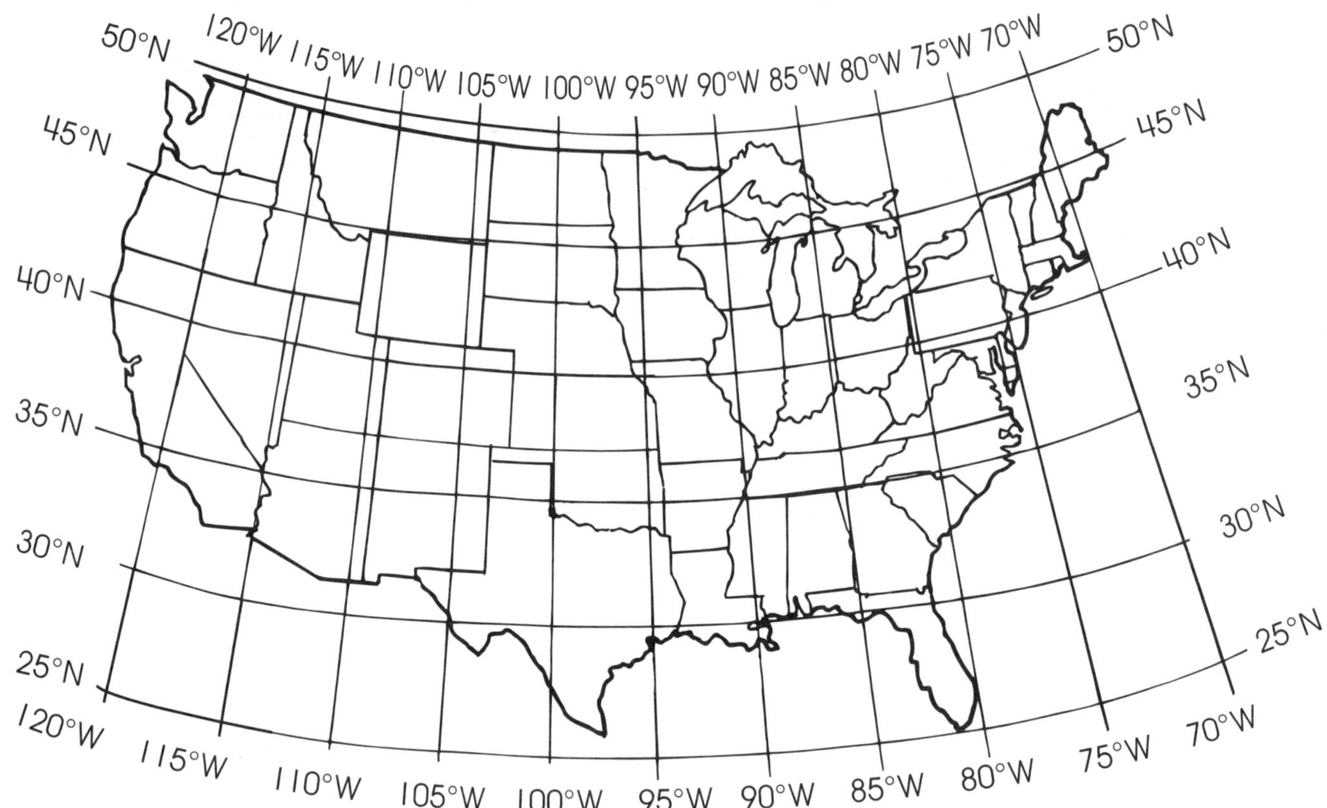

	Latitude	Longitude	State	Color
1.	45°N / 50°N	105°W / 115°W	__________	orange
2.	40°N / 45°N	75°W / 80°W	__________	tan
3.	44°N / 50°N	67°W / 70°W	__________	red
4.	25°N / 30°N	80°W / 85°W	__________	yellow
5.	40°N / 45°N	90°W / 95°W	__________	gray
6.	30°N / 35°N	85°W / 90°W	__________	green
7.	43°N / 47°N	87°W / 93°W	__________	blue
8.	31°N / 36°N	104°W / 109°W	__________	pink
9.	36°N / 38°N	82°W / 89°W	__________	lt. green
10.	36°N / 39°N	76°W / 84°W	__________	gold
11.	26°N / 34°N	94°W / 107°W	__________	purple
12.	41°N / 45°N	104°W / 111°W	__________	lt. blue
13.	36°N / 41°N	90°W / 95°W	__________	brown

See the U.S.A.

Use the coordinates to plan a trip across the U.S.A.

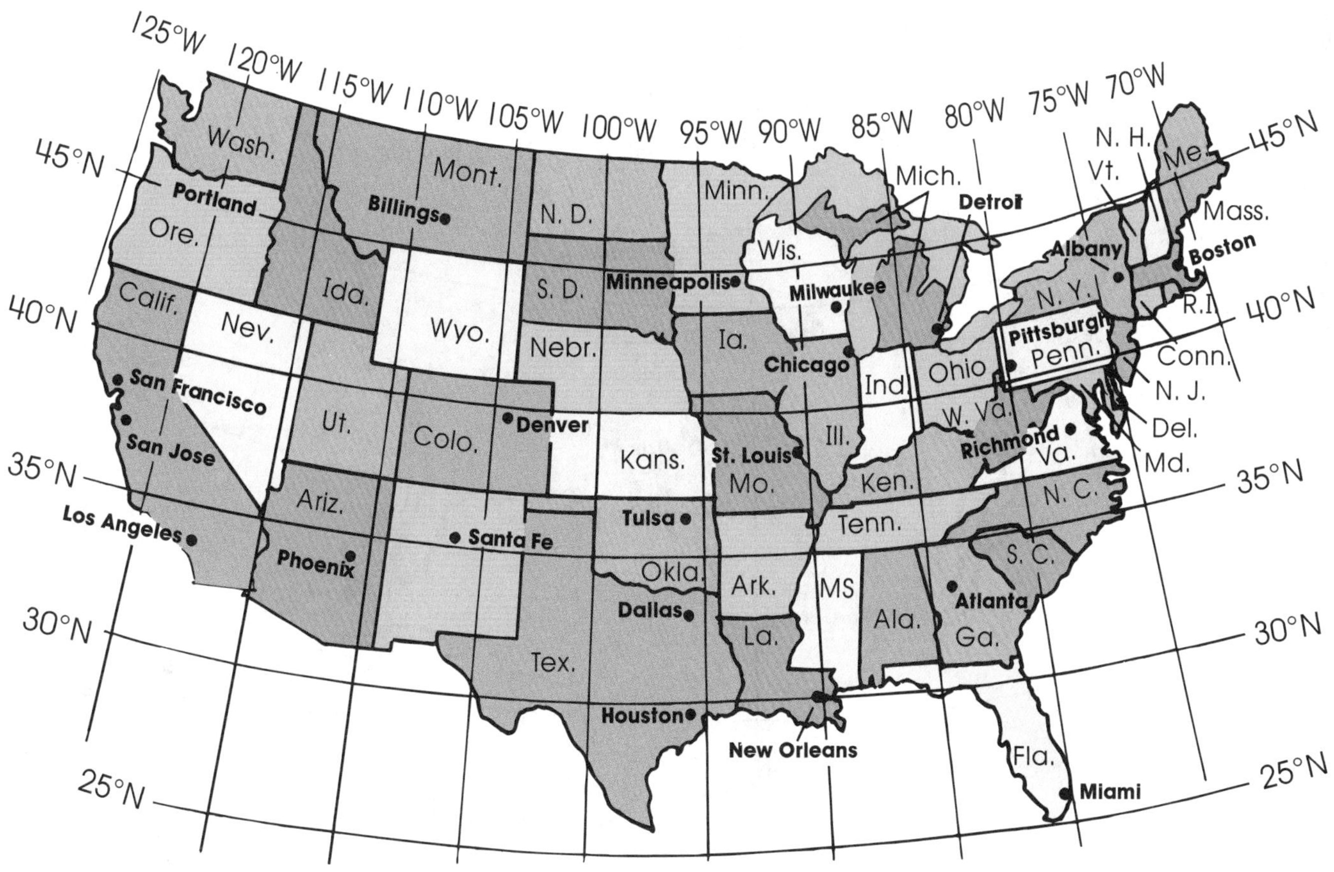

Directions: Write the name of the city closest to the intersection.

1. Your trip begins at 40°N / 105°W, the Mile-High City. ______________
2. You fly over the Rocky Mountains to 45°N / 125°W. ______________
3. Now, to 35°N / 105°W in New Mexico. ______________
4. Next, stop is Texas, the city of . . . 30°N / 95°W. ______________
5. It's Mardi Gras time at 30°N / 90°W. ______________
6. Then, fun in the sun and the Atlantic Ocean 25°N / 80°W. ______________
7. To the Gateway Arch in the city of . . 40°N / 90°W. ______________
8. The Steelers play football here—40°N / 80°W. ______________
9. Next, to the capital of New York—40°N / 75°W. ______________

Plotting North American Cities

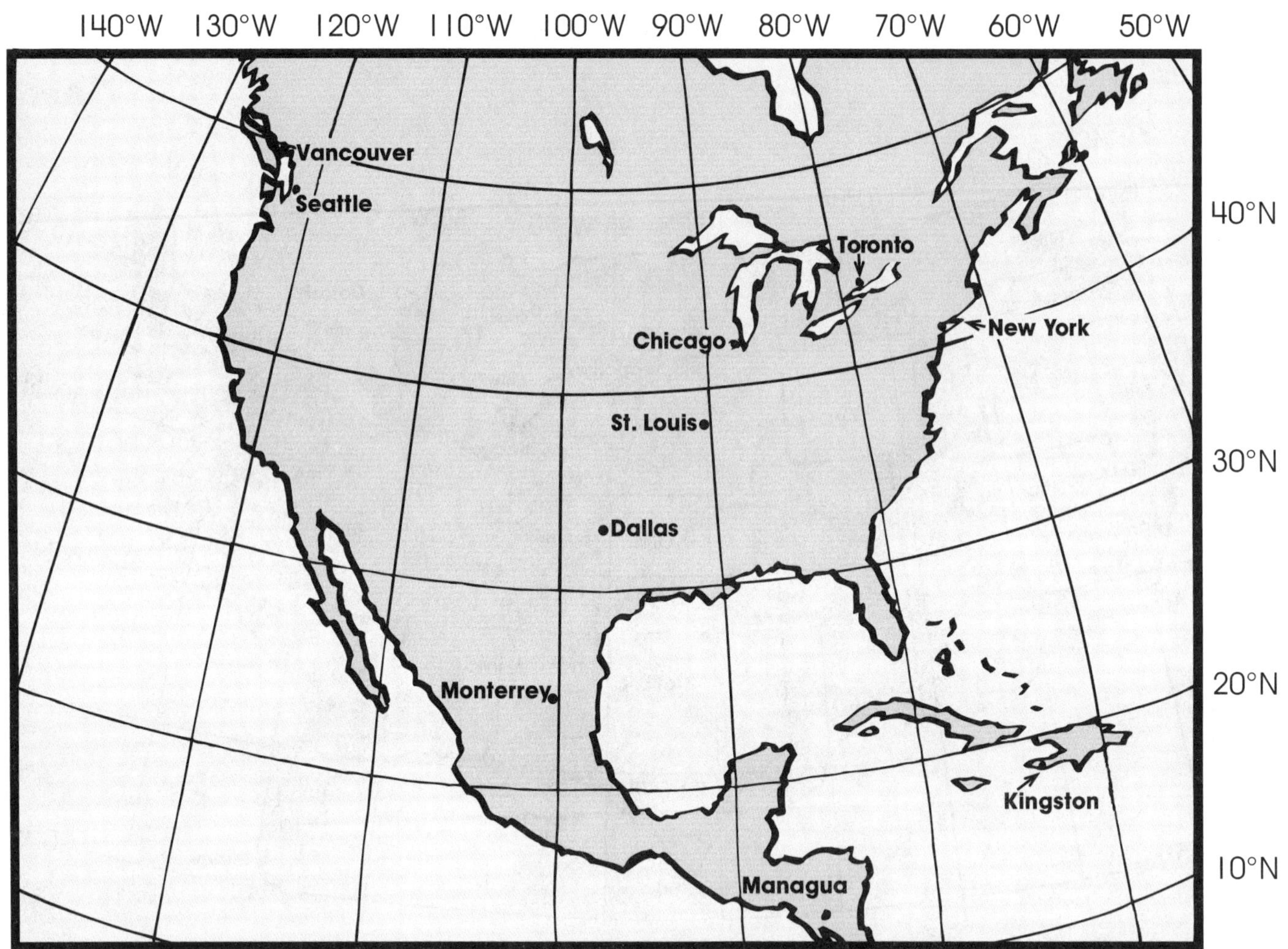

Directions: Use the lines of latitude and longitude to determine the approximate coordinates of the North American cities on the map above. Write the coordinates for each city in the blanks.

	Latitude	**Longitude**		**Latitude**	**Longitude**
1. Seattle	________	________	6. St. Louis	________	________
2. Kingston	________	________	7. Toronto	________	________
3. Dallas	________	________	8. New York	________	________
4. Vancouver	________	________	9. Monterrey	________	________
5. Managua	________	________	10. Chicago	________	________

Batter Up!

Directions: Use the coordinates below and the map on page 56 to locate these cities. Then, unscramble the words to find out the baseball teams which call these cities "home base."

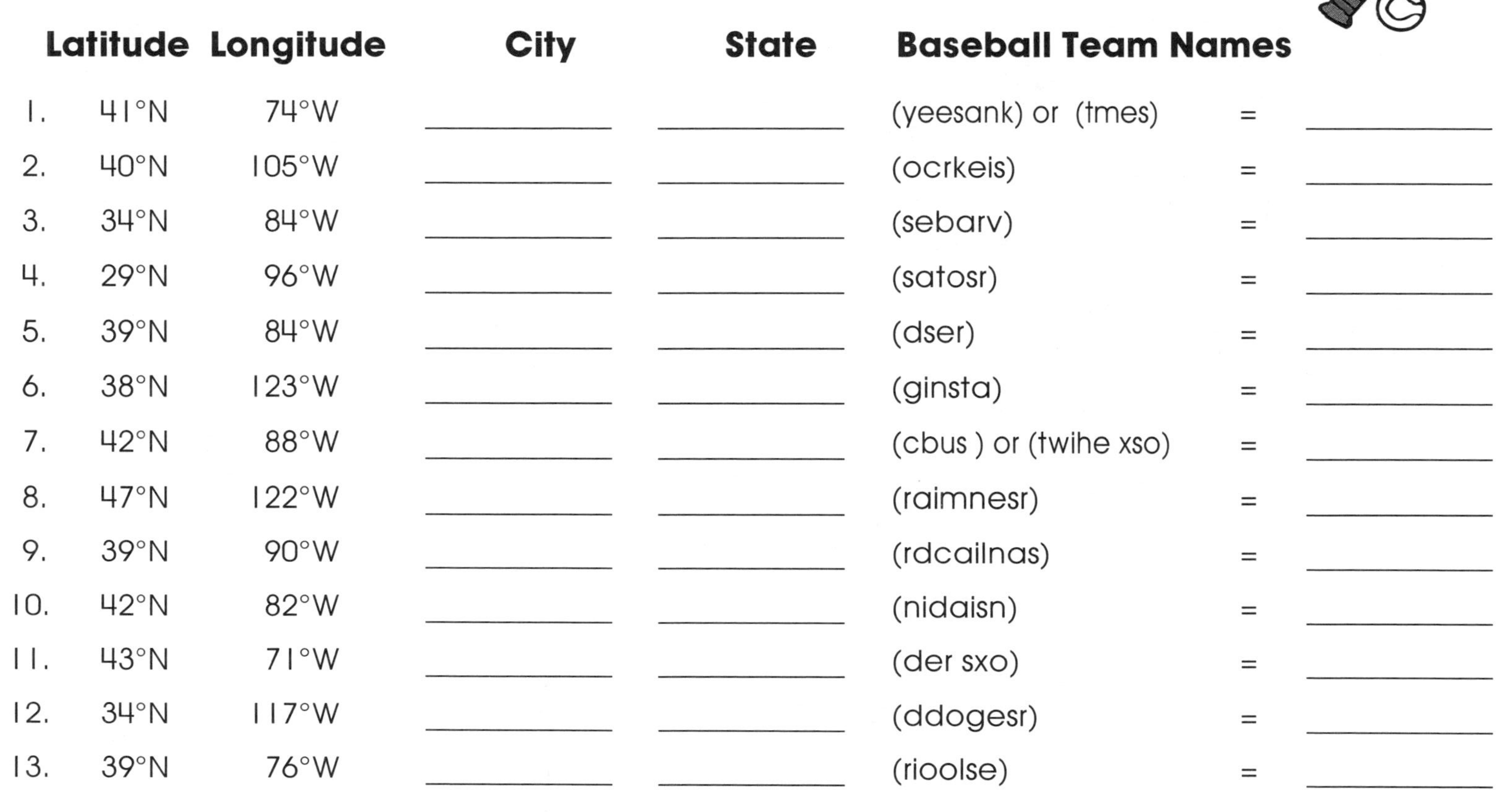

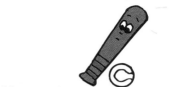

	Latitude	Longitude	City	State	Baseball Team Names		
1.	41°N	74°W	______	______	(yeesank) or (tmes)	=	______
2.	40°N	105°W	______	______	(ocrkeis)	=	______
3.	34°N	84°W	______	______	(sebarv)	=	______
4.	29°N	96°W	______	______	(satosr)	=	______
5.	39°N	84°W	______	______	(dser)	=	______
6.	38°N	123°W	______	______	(ginsta)	=	______
7.	42°N	88°W	______	______	(cbus) or (twihe xso)	=	______
8.	47°N	122°W	______	______	(raimnesr)	=	______
9.	39°N	90°W	______	______	(rdcailnas)	=	______
10.	42°N	82°W	______	______	(nidaisn)	=	______
11.	43°N	71°W	______	______	(der sxo)	=	______
12.	34°N	117°W	______	______	(ddogesr)	=	______
13.	39°N	76°W	______	______	(rioolse)	=	______

Word Bank

Orioles, Indians, Cardinals, Dodgers, Giants, Rockies, Cubs, White Sox, Yankees, Astros, Mets, Braves, Reds, Mariners, Red Sox

Batter Up!

San Francisco
Los Angeles
Seattle
Denver
Houston
St. Louis
Chicago
Cincinnati
Cleveland
Atlanta
New York City
Baltimore
Boston
CA
OR
WA
NV
ID
AZ
UT
MT
WY
NM
CO
NE
SD
ND
TX
OK
KS
IA
MN
LA
AK
MO
WI
IL
MS
TN
IN
MI
AL
KY
OH
GA
SC
WV
FL
NC
VA
PA
NY
VT
NH
ME
MD
DE
NJ
CT
RI
MA
125°W
120°W
115°W
110°W
105°W
100°W
95°W
90°W
85°W
80°W
75°W
70°W
25°N
30°N
35°N
40°N
45°N
50°N
N
S
E
W

Four States

Directions: Use this map to fill in the charts on page 58. Two answers have been filled in for you.

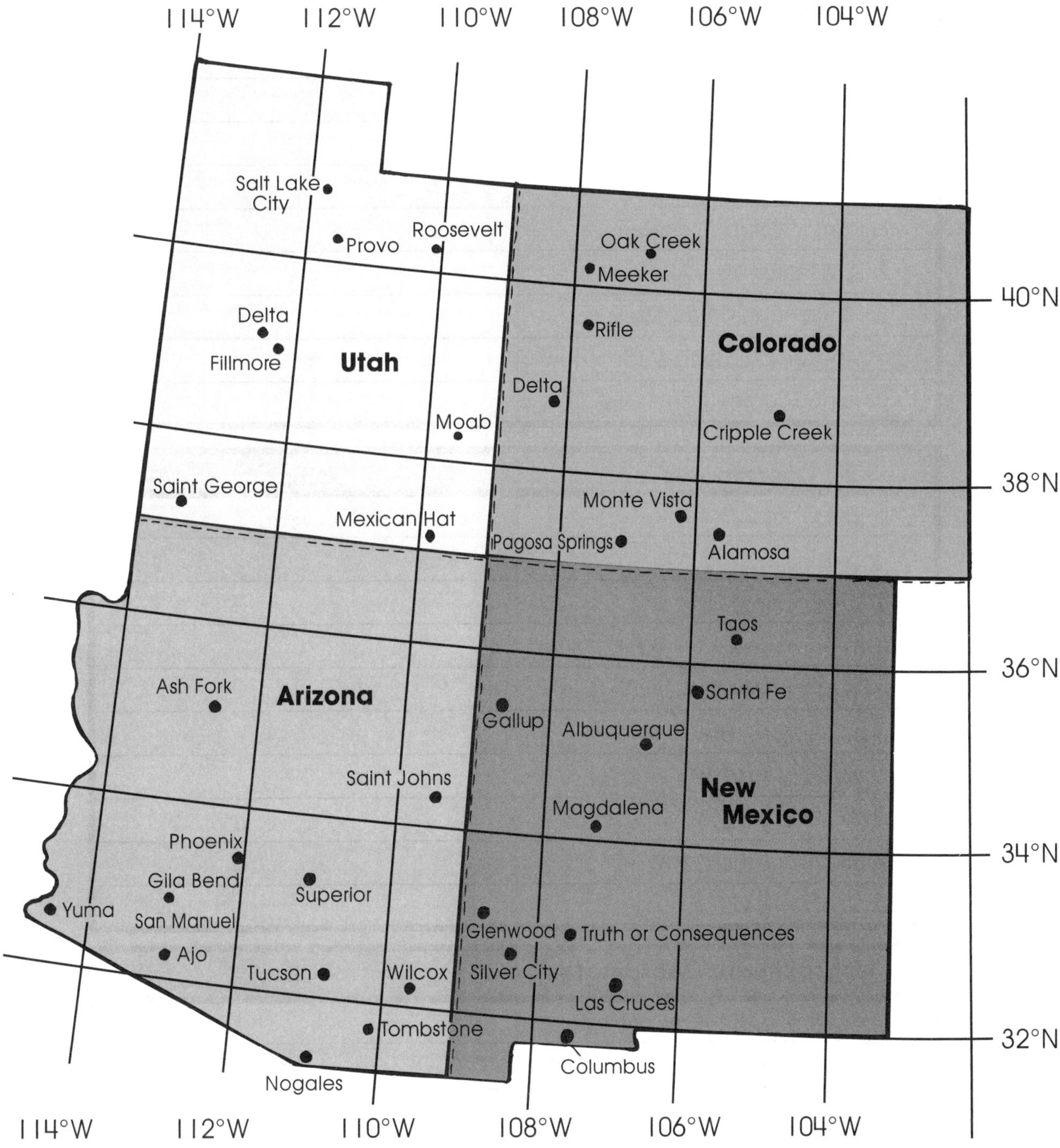

Four States

Use with page 57.

City	Coordinates
1. Salt Lake City, Utah	41°N / 112°W
2. Tucson, Arizona	
3. Santa Fe, New Mexico	
4. Oak Creek, Colorado	
5. Wilcox, Arizona	
6. Cripple Creek, Colorado	
7. Las Cruces, New Mexico	
8. Albuquerque, New Mexico	
9. Meeker, Colorado	
10. Saint George, Utah	

Coordinates	City
1. 33°N / 109°W	Glenwood
2. 41°N / 112°W	
3. 39°N / 108°W	
4. 31°N / 111°W	
5. 37°N / 110°W	
6. 40 1/2°N / 110°W	
7. 33 1/2°N / 107°W	
8. 39°N / 112 1/2°W	
9. 35 1/2°N / 108 1/2°W	
10. 33°N / 111°W	

Approximate Coordinates	State
32°N / 36°N and 110°W / 114°W	
36°N / 40°N and 110°W / 114°W	
32°N / 36°N and 104°W / 108°W	
36°N / 40°N and 104°W / 108°W	

Name the City

Directions: Use the coordinates given below to locate each of the cities. The first one has been done for you.

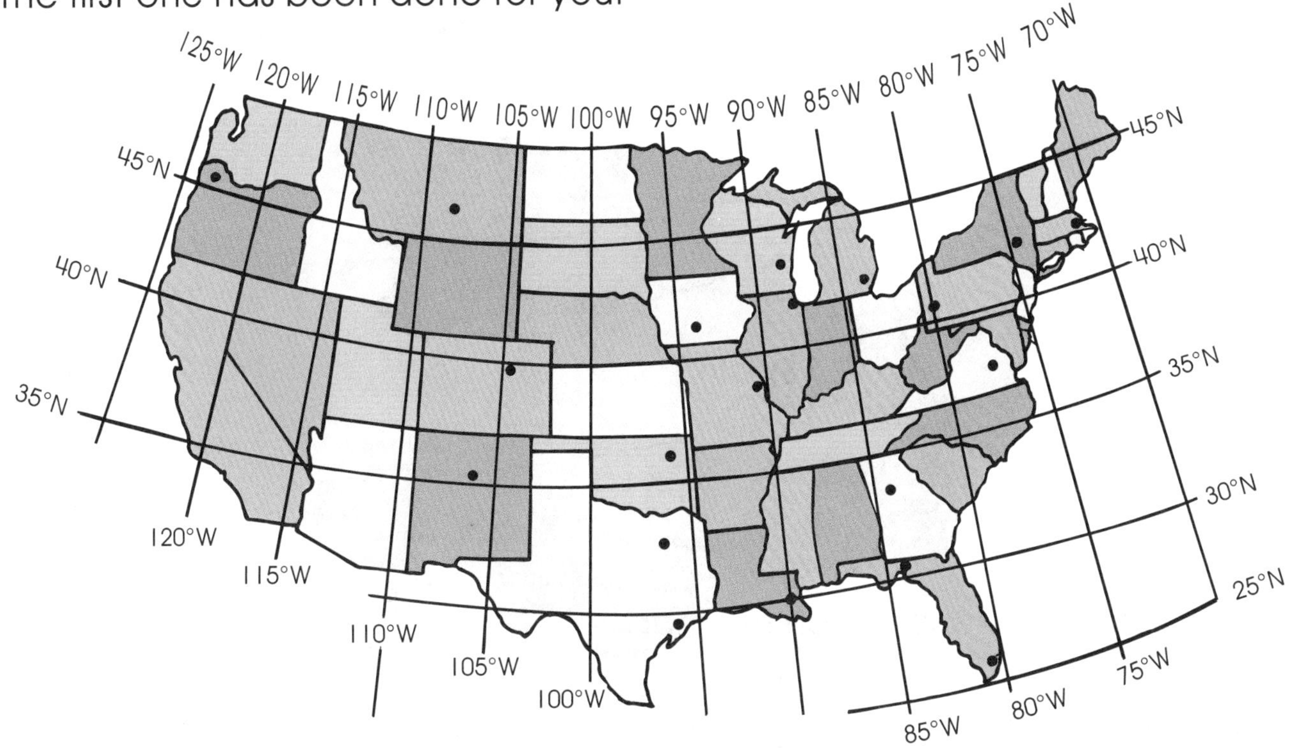

Latitude	Longitude	City
1. 34°N	84°W	Atlanta
2. 26°N	80°W	
3. 40°N	80°W	
4. 36°N	96°W	
5. 37°N	122°W	
6. 33°N	112°W	
7. 39°N	90°W	
8. 46°N	108°W	
9. 43°N	88°W	
10. 42°N	94°W	
11. 43°N	74°W	
12. 45°N	93°W	
13. 33°N	97°W	
14. 30°N	95°W	

Locating Places in Western Europe

1. Name the four countries on this map.

   ________________ ________________ ________________ ________________

2. One inch equals ______________ miles on the map.
3. Which parallel line crosses both Portugal and Spain? ________________
4. Which two parallel lines cross France? ________________ ______________
5. Name the country directly north of France. ________________________
6. Place the city of Barcelona on the northeastern coast of Spain about 225 miles south of the 45°N parallel.
7. Place the city of Paris in the north-central part of France about 75 miles south of the 50°N parallel.
8. Place Lisbon on the western coast of Portugal about 75 miles south of the 40°N parallel.
9. Place Madrid in the center of Spain about 50 miles north of the 40°N parallel.
10. Place Brussels near the northcentral part of Belgium about 50 miles north of the 50°N parallel line.
11. Place Toulouse in the southwestern part of France 100 miles south of the 45°N parallel.

Where in Europe?

Use with page 62.

Where in Europe?

Directions: Estimate and write the coordinates and countries for these European cities using the map on page 61. The first one has been done for you.

City	Latitude	Longitude	Country
1. London	52°N	0°	United Kingdom
2. Belgrade			
3. Warsaw			
4. Stockholm			
5. Athens			
6. Helsinki			
7. Paris			
8. Munich			
9. Copenhagen			
10. Oslo			
11. Glasgow			
12. Prague			
13. Bern			
14. Hamburg			
15. Dresden			
16. Dublin			
17. Rome			
18. Budapest			
19. Vienna			
20. Amsterdam			

Latitude and Longitude Lines

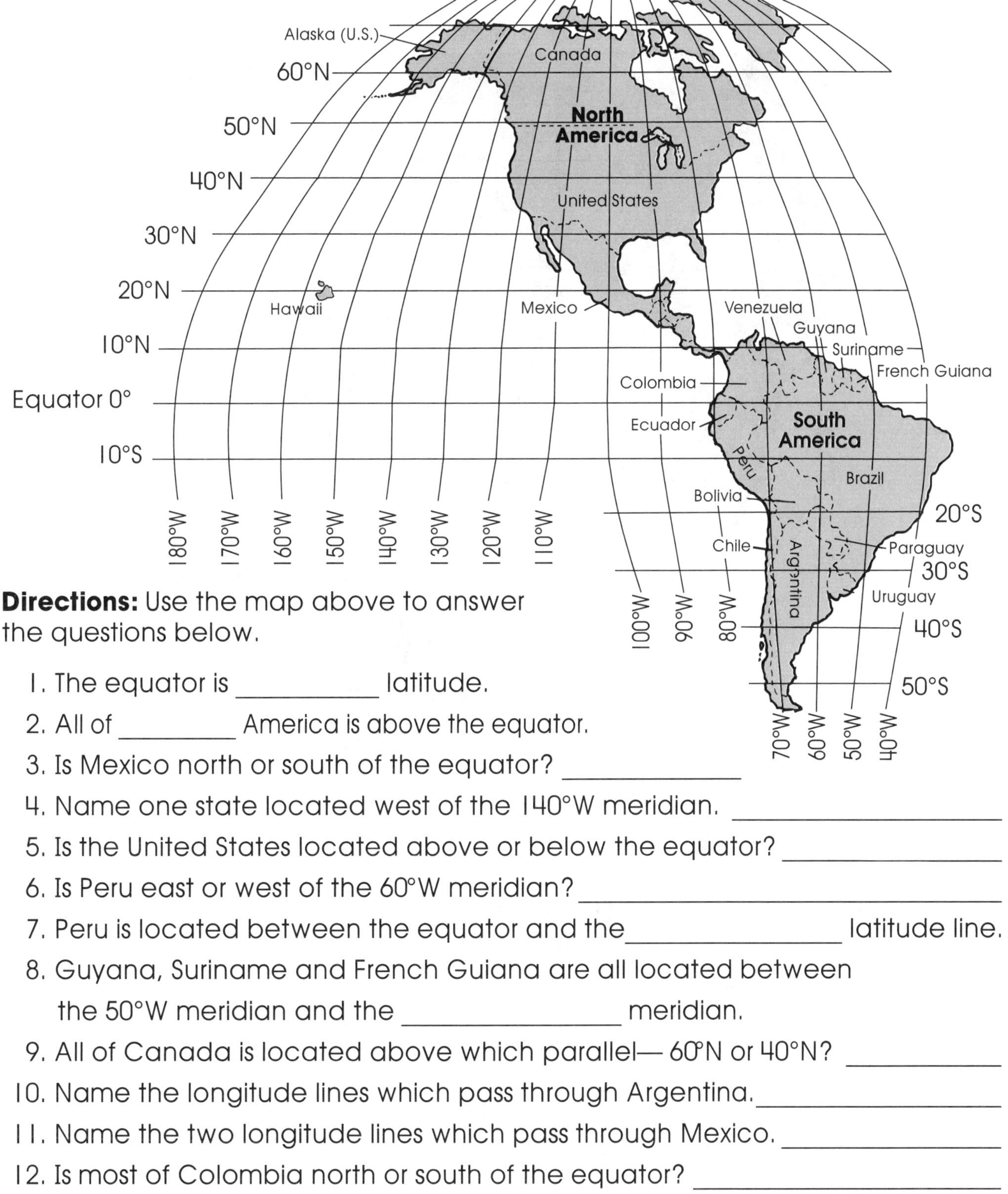

Directions: Use the map above to answer the questions below.

1. The equator is ___________ latitude.
2. All of _________ America is above the equator.
3. Is Mexico north or south of the equator? ____________
4. Name one state located west of the 140°W meridian. ______________
5. Is the United States located above or below the equator? ______________
6. Is Peru east or west of the 60°W meridian? ______________
7. Peru is located between the equator and the ______________ latitude line.
8. Guyana, Suriname and French Guiana are all located between the 50°W meridian and the ______________ meridian.
9. All of Canada is located above which parallel— 60°N or 40°N? __________
10. Name the longitude lines which pass through Argentina. ______________
11. Name the two longitude lines which pass through Mexico. ______________
12. Is most of Colombia north or south of the equator? ______________

Pinpointing North American Cities

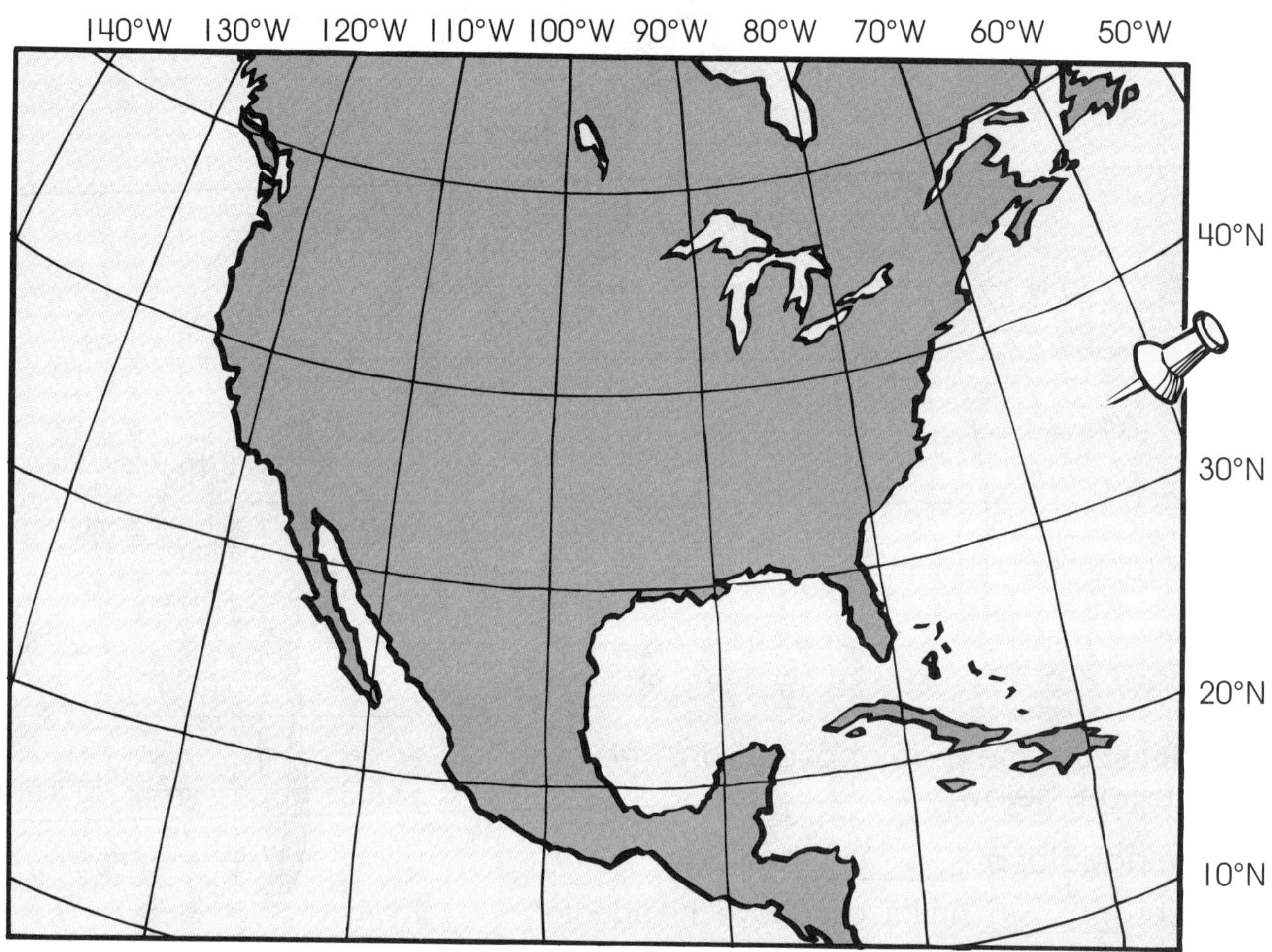

Use a globe or map to identify the city that is located at each set of coordinates. Write the name of the city on the blank and in the correct location on the map. There may be some slight variance in the degrees.

	City	Latitude	Longitude		City	Latitude	Longitude
1.	____________	25°N	80°W	6.	____________	19°N	99°W
2.	____________	39°N	104°W	7.	____________	51°N	114°W
3.	____________	50°N	97°W	8.	____________	33°N	84°W
4.	____________	23°N	82°W	9.	____________	42°N	83°W
5.	____________	37°N	122°W	10.	____________	46°N	71°W

Night and Day Difference

What causes the daily change from daylight to darkness? Day turns into night because the earth rotates, or spins, on its axis. The earth's axis is an imaginary line that cuts through the earth from the North Pole to the South Pole. The earth spins in a counter-clockwise direction.

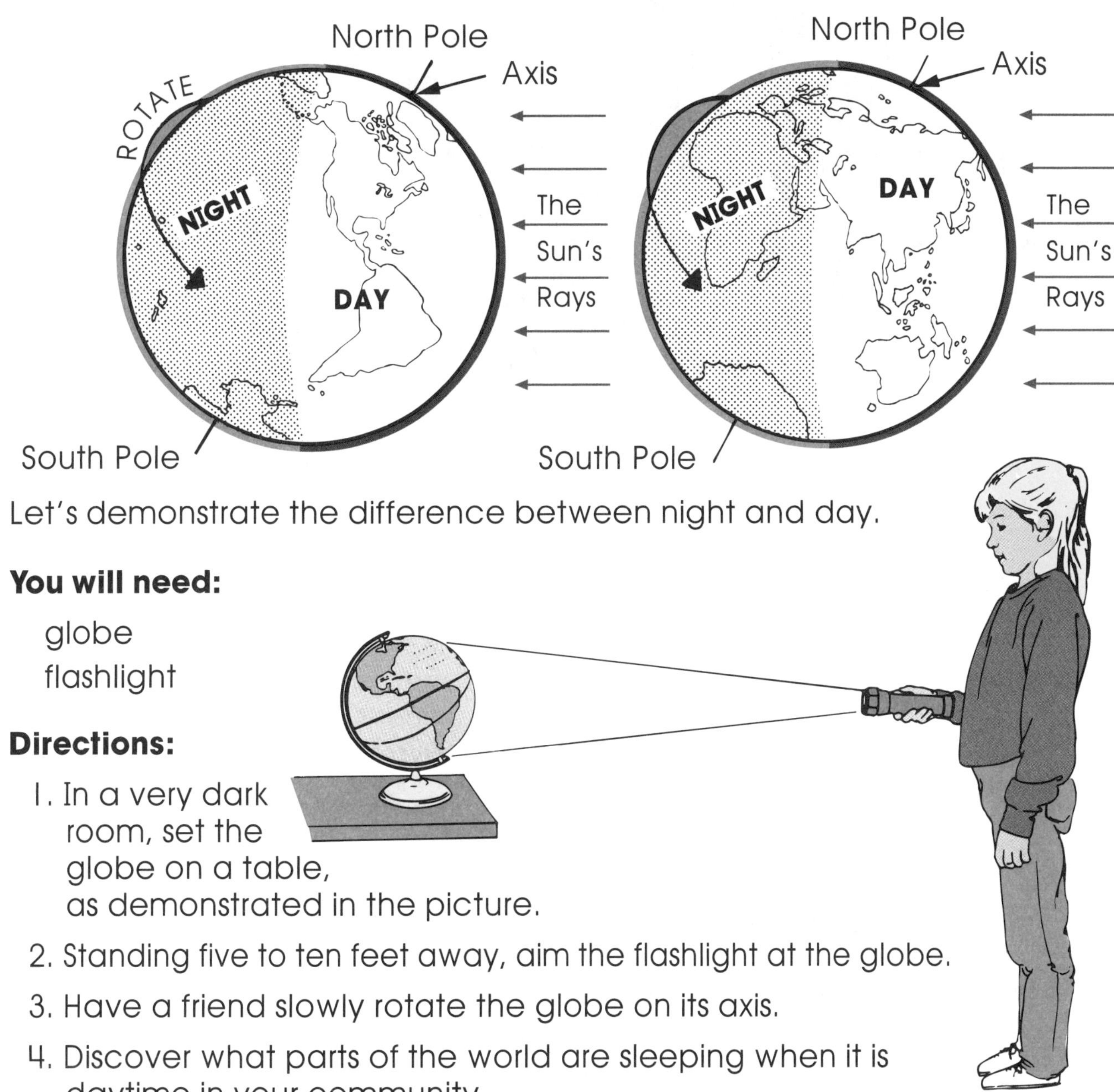

Let's demonstrate the difference between night and day.

You will need:

globe
flashlight

Directions:

1. In a very dark room, set the globe on a table, as demonstrated in the picture.
2. Standing five to ten feet away, aim the flashlight at the globe.
3. Have a friend slowly rotate the globe on its axis.
4. Discover what parts of the world are sleeping when it is daytime in your community.

Do You Have the Time?

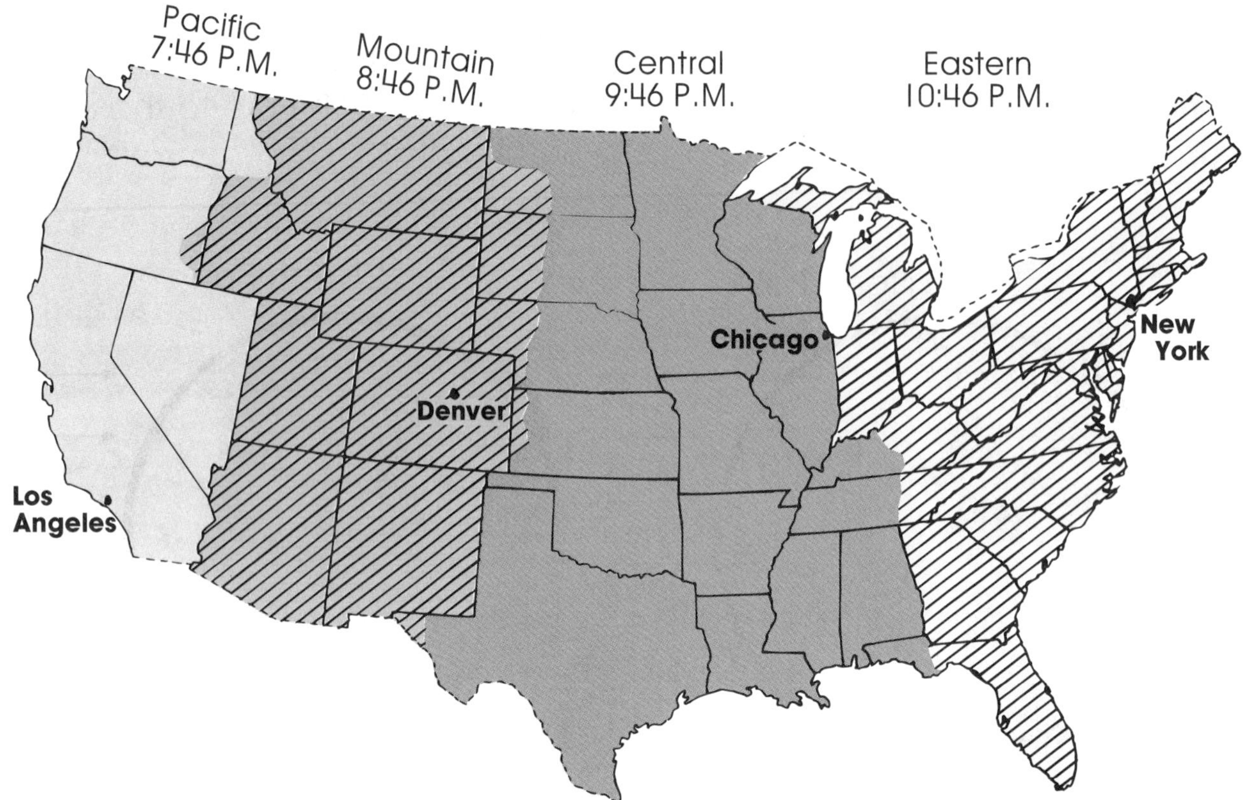

The earth spins on its axis in a west to east direction. This causes our day to begin with the sun rising in the east and setting in the west. Different areas of the United States can have different amounts of daylight at the same moment in time. For instance, when the sun is rising in New York, it is still dark in California.

A **time zone** is an area in which everyone has the same time. Every zone is one hour different from its neighbor. There are 24 time zones around the world. There are six time zones in the United States. The map above shows the four zones that cover the 48 contiguous, or touching, states.

When it is 6 o'clock in New York, what time is it in . . .

Chicago?__________ Los Angeles?____________ Denver?_____________

What is the name of the time zone in which you live? ________________

Name three other states in your time zone.

____________________ ____________________ ____________________

World Time Zones

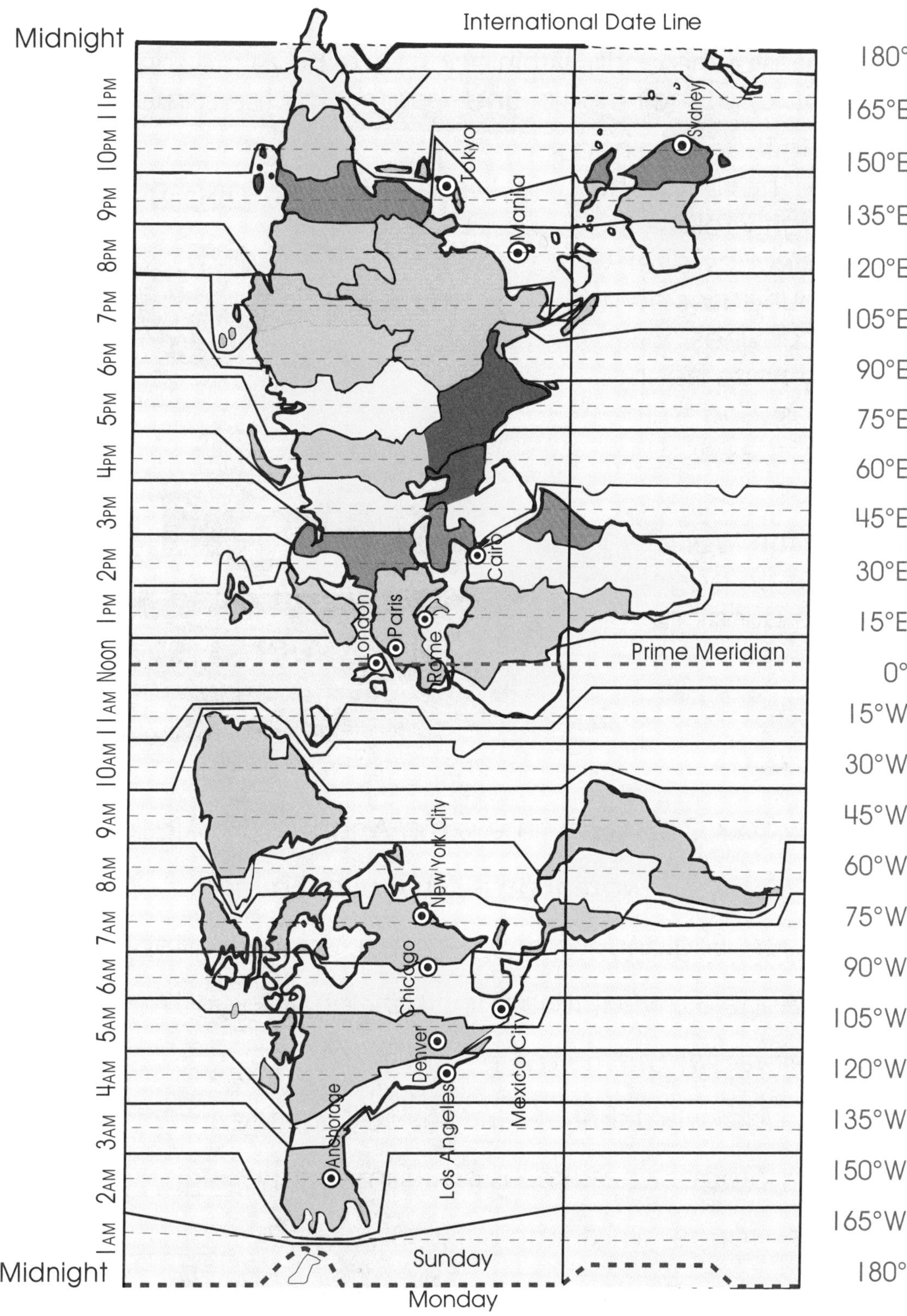

Use with page 68.

24-Hour Globe

The earth is divided into 24 standard time zones. These time zones are set so that large sections of the earth within each zone have the same time. In each time zone, people set their clocks and watches by the same time.

Every 15° of longitude begins a new time zone. The time zone boundaries roughly follow the lines of longitude. However, many of the boundaries do not follow exactly the lines of longitude. They have been altered to correspond to the boundaries of states and countries.

Directions: Use the World Time Zones map on page 67 to answer the questions below.

If it is . . .

3 A.M. in New York City, what time is it in Anchorage, Alaska? __________

4 P.M. in Tokyo, Japan, what time is it in Cairo, Egypt? __________

1 P.M. in London, England, what time is it in Manila, Philippines? __________

3 P.M. in Los Angeles, what time is it in London, England? __________

10 A.M. in Denver, what time is it in Paris, France? __________

9 P.M. in Chicago, what time is it in Mexico City, Mexico? __________

4 A.M. in Anchorage, what time is it in Rome, Italy? __________

1 P.M. in Paris, France, what time is it in Chicago? __________

11 P.M. in New York City, what time is it in Paris, France? __________

Changing Times

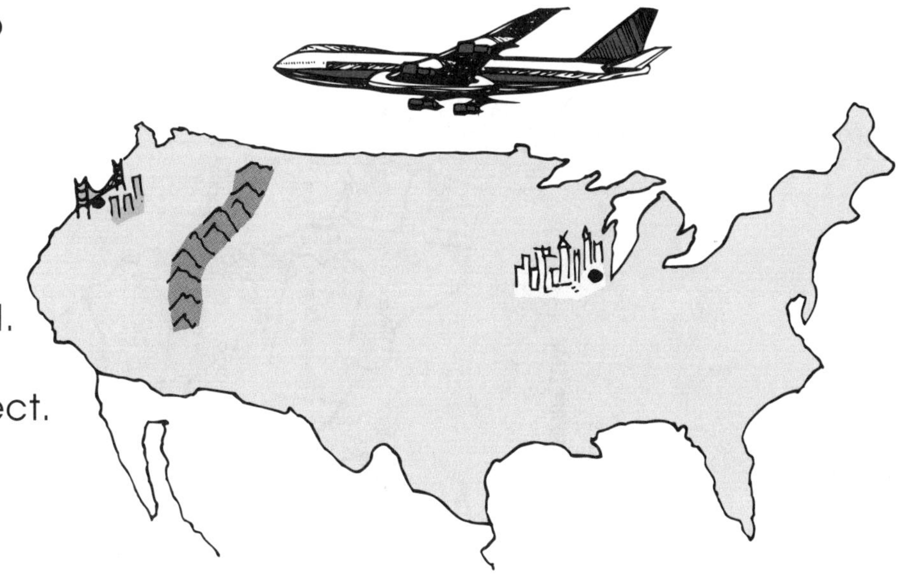

A plane leaves Chicago at 5:30 P.M. heading for San Francisco. The flight takes 3 hours. At what time will it arrive in San Francisco?

If you answered 8:30 P.M. to the above question, you are only partly correct. It would be 8:30 P.M. "Chicago time" but it would be 6:30 P.M. in San Francisco because the plane crossed two time zones.

Examine the time zones of the United States on the map on page 70. Notice that the time-zone boundaries do not always follow the state boundaries. Some states are in more than one time zone.

Directions: Use the United States Time Zones map (page 70) to answer the following questions.

1. How many time zones are there in the United States? ______________
2. How many time zones are there in the 48 contiguous (touching) states?

   ____

3. Name the time zones in all 50 states.______________________________

   ____

4. If it is 3:30 P.M. in your state, what time is it in . . .

   California? ____________________ Iowa?______________________

   New York?______________________ Colorado? ________________

5. What time is it right now in . . .

   Miami, Florida? ________________ Portland, Oregon?____________

   Grand Rapids, Michigan? _______ Dallas, Texas? ________________

   Cody, Wyoming? _______________ Richmond, Virginia? __________

United States Time Zones

Use with page 69.

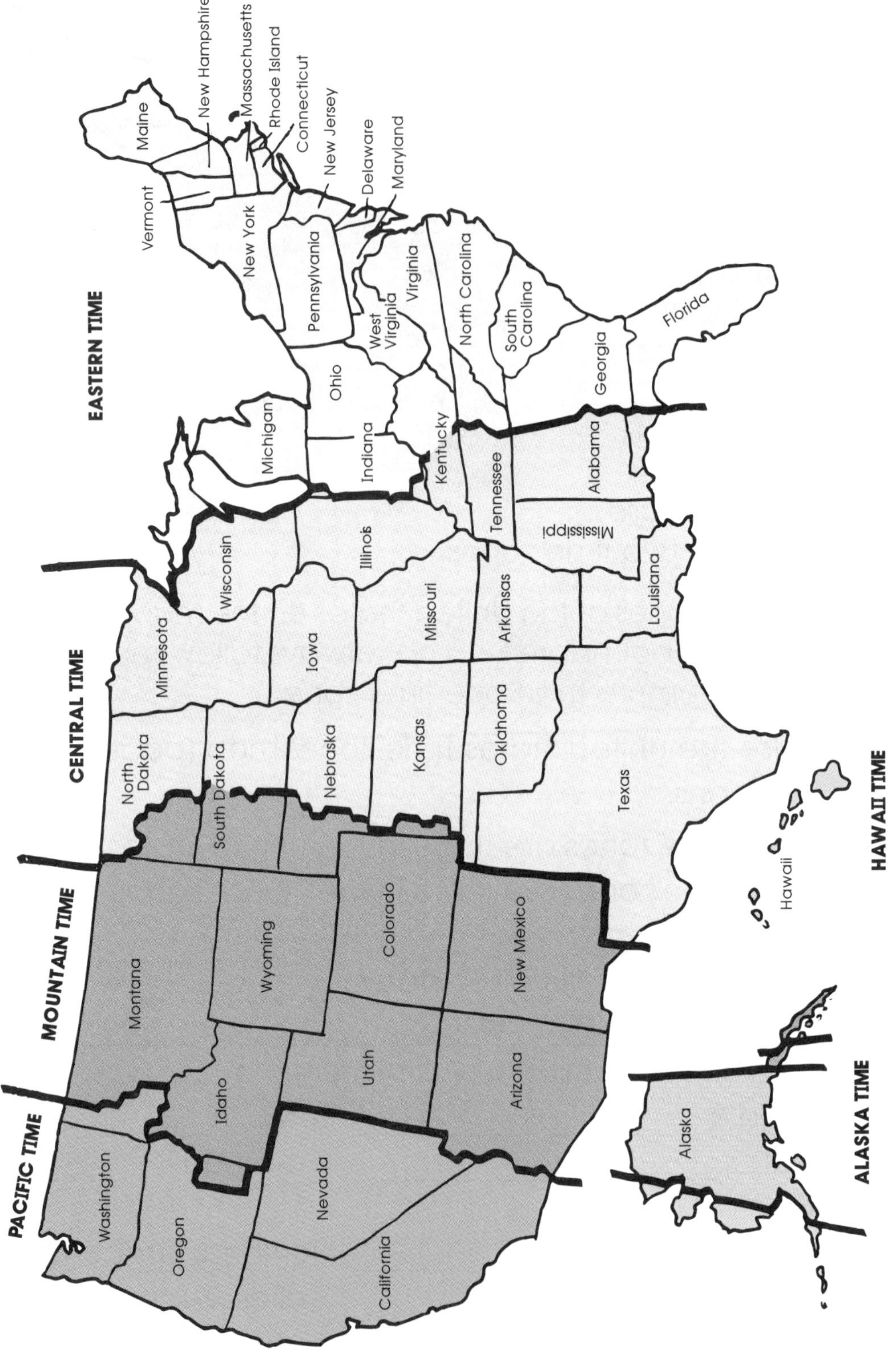

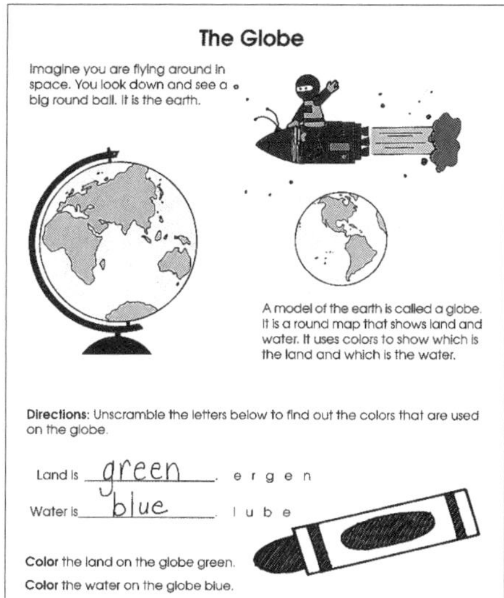

The Globe

Imagine you are flying around in space. You look down and see a big round ball. It is the earth.

A model of the earth is called a globe. It is a round map that shows land and water. It uses colors to show which is the land and which is the water.

Directions: Unscramble the letters below to find out the colors that are used on the globe.

Land is green . e r g e n

Water is blue . l u b e

Color the land on the globe green.

Color the water on the globe blue.

Page 6

It's a Round World

The picture of the globe on page 253 shows both halves of the world. It shows the large pieces of land called continents. There are seven continents. Find them on the globe.

Directions: Write the names of the seven continents.

1. North America
2. South America
3. Europe
4. Africa
5. Asia
6. Australia
7. Antarctica

There are four bodies of water called oceans. Find the oceans on the globe. Write the names below.

1. Atlantic
2. Pacific
3. Indian
4. Arctic

Page 8

A Global Guide

Use the globe on page 253. Read the clues below. Write the answers on the lines. Then, use the numbered letters to solve the riddle at the bottom of the page.

1. This direction points up. north
2. This direction points down. south
3. This direction points right. east
4. This direction points left. west
5. This ocean is west of North America. Pacific Ocean
6. This ocean is south of Asia. Indian Ocean
7. This ocean is east of South America. Atlantic Ocean

Riddle: What does a globe do? It spins us around our planet.

Page 9

Land and Water

Directions: Use the map below plus a wall map to do this activity.

Write the name of each continent in the correct blank.

1. South America
2. Africa
3. Asia
4. North America
5. Antarctica
6. Australia
7. Europe

Write the name of each ocean in the correct blank.

A. Arctic
B. Pacific
C. Atlantic
D. Indian

Use crayons or markers to follow these directions.

1. Color Australia green.
2. Color Europe yellow.
3. Color Africa orange.
4. Color Antarctica blue.
5. Color North America red.
6. Color South America brown.
7. Color Asia purple.

Page 10

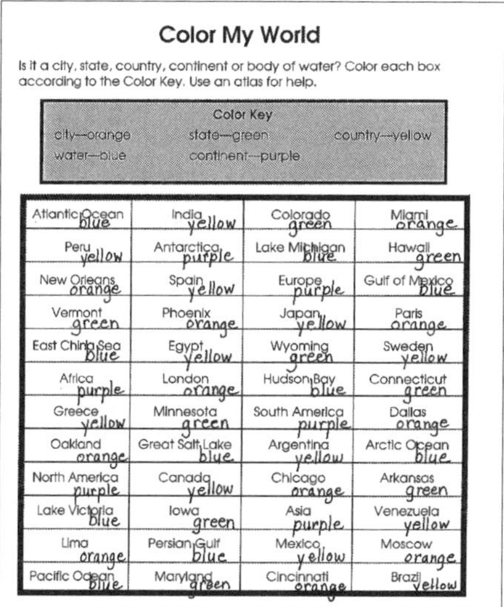

Color My World

Is it a city, state, country, continent or body of water? Color each box according to the Color Key. Use an atlas for help.

Color Key
city—orange state—green country—yellow
water—blue continent—purple

Atlantic Ocean blue	India yellow	Colorado green	Miami orange
Peru yellow	Antarctica purple	Lake Michigan blue	Hawaii green
New Orleans orange	Spain yellow	Europe purple	Gulf of Mexico blue
Vermont green	Phoenix orange	Japan yellow	Paris orange
East China Sea blue	Egypt yellow	Wyoming green	Sweden yellow
Africa purple	London orange	Hudson Bay blue	Connecticut green
Greece yellow	Minnesota green	South America purple	Dallas orange
Oakland orange	Great Salt Lake blue	Argentina yellow	Arctic Ocean blue
North America purple	Canada yellow	Chicago orange	Arkansas green
Lake Victoria blue	Iowa green	Asia purple	Venezuela yellow
Lima orange	Persian Gulf blue	Mexico yellow	Moscow orange
Pacific Ocean blue	Maryland green	Cincinnati orange	Brazil yellow

Page 11

Where in the World Is. . .

What is your global address? It's more than your street, city, state and ZIP code.

What would your address be if you wanted to get a letter from a friend living in outer space?

Use an atlas, encyclopedia, science book or other source to complete your global address.

Inter-Galactic Address Book

Name ________________

Street Answers

County or Parish will

State or Province vary.

Country ________________

Continent ________________

Hemisphere ________________

Planet ________________

Galaxy ________________

Draw an **X** to mark the approximate place where you live.

Page 12

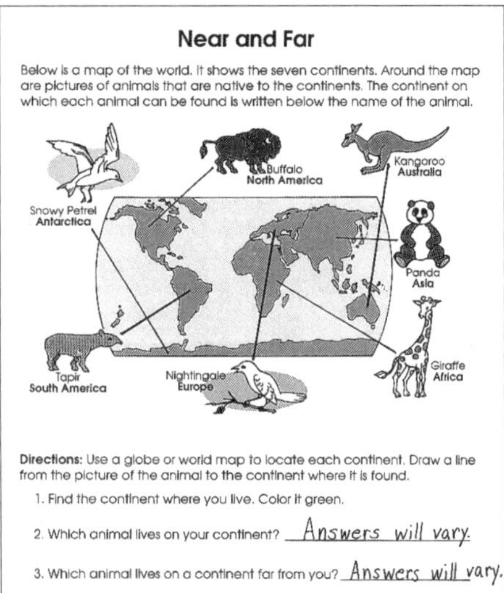

Near and Far

Below is a map of the world. It shows the seven continents. Around the map are pictures of animals that are native to the continents. The continent on which each animal can be found is written below the name of the animal.

Directions: Use a globe or world map to locate each continent. Draw a line from the picture of the animal to the continent where it is found.

1. Find the continent where you live. Color it green.
2. Which animal lives on your continent? Answers will vary.
3. Which animal lives on a continent far from you? Answers will vary.

Page 19

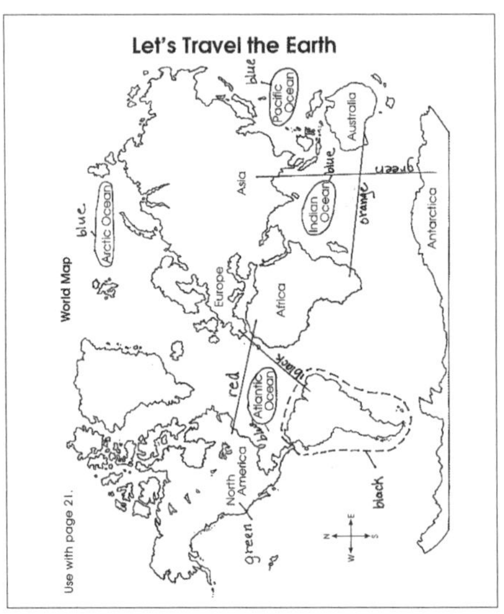

Let's Travel the Earth

Page 20

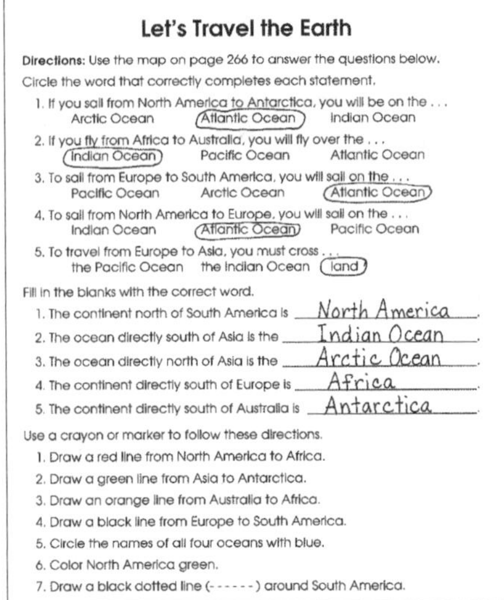

Let's Travel the Earth

Directions: Use the map on page 266 to answer the questions below.

Circle the word that correctly completes each statement.

1. If you sail from North America to Antarctica, you will be on the . . .
   Arctic Ocean (Atlantic Ocean) Indian Ocean
2. If you fly from Africa to Australia, you will fly over the . . .
   (Indian Ocean) Pacific Ocean Atlantic Ocean
3. To sail from Europe to South America, you will sail on the . . .
   Pacific Ocean Arctic Ocean (Atlantic Ocean)
4. To sail from North America to Europe, you will sail on the . . .
   Indian Ocean (Atlantic Ocean) Pacific Ocean
5. To travel from Europe to Asia, you must cross . . .
   the Pacific Ocean the Indian Ocean (land)

Fill in the blanks with the correct word.

1. The continent north of South America is North America.
2. The ocean directly south of Asia is the Indian Ocean.
3. The ocean directly north of Asia is the Arctic Ocean.
4. The continent directly south of Europe is Africa.
5. The continent directly south of Australia is Antarctica.

Use a crayon or marker to follow these directions.

1. Draw a red line from North America to Africa.
2. Draw a green line from Asia to Antarctica.
3. Draw an orange line from Australia to Africa.
4. Draw a black line from Europe to South America.
5. Circle the names of all four oceans with blue.
6. Color North America green.
7. Draw a black dotted line (- - - - - -) around South America.

Page 21

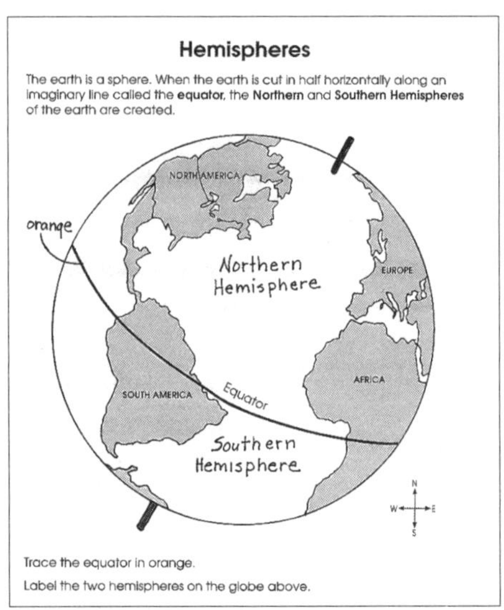

Hemispheres

The earth is a sphere. When the earth is cut in half horizontally along an imaginary line called the **equator**, the **Northern** and **Southern Hemispheres** of the earth are created.

Trace the equator in orange.

Label the two hemispheres on the globe above.

Page 22

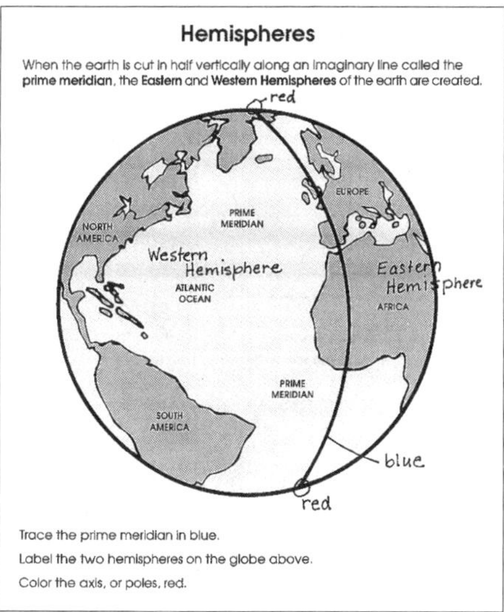

Hemispheres

When the earth is cut in half vertically along an imaginary line called the **prime meridian**, the **Eastern** and **Western Hemispheres** of the earth are created.

Trace the prime meridian in blue.

Label the two hemispheres on the globe above.

Color the axis, or poles, red.

Page 23

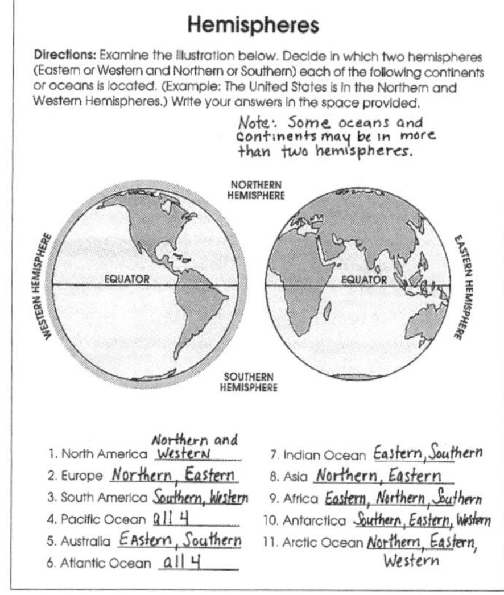

Hemispheres

Directions: Examine the illustration below. Decide in which two hemispheres (Eastern or Western and Northern or Southern) each of the following continents or oceans is located. (Example: The United States is in the Northern and Western Hemispheres.) Write your answers in the space provided.

Note: Some oceans and continents may be in more than two hemispheres.

1. North America Northern and Western
2. Europe Northern, Eastern
3. South America Southern, Western
4. Pacific Ocean all 4
5. Australia Eastern, Southern
6. Atlantic Ocean all 4
7. Indian Ocean Eastern, Southern
8. Asia Northern, Eastern
9. Africa Eastern, Northern, Southern
10. Antarctica Southern, Eastern, Western
11. Arctic Ocean Northern, Eastern, Western

Page 24

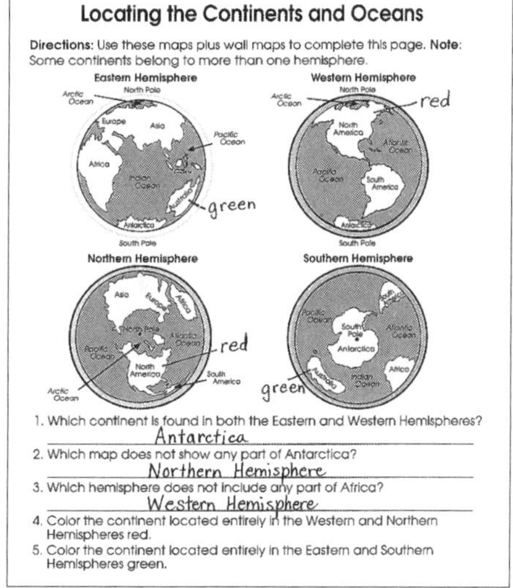

Locating the Continents and Oceans

Directions: Use these maps plus wall maps to complete this page. **Note:** Some continents belong to more than one hemisphere.

1. Which continent is found in both the Eastern and Western Hemispheres? Antarctica
2. Which map does not show any part of Antarctica? Northern Hemisphere
3. Which hemisphere does not include any part of Africa? Western Hemisphere
4. Color the continent located entirely in the Western and Northern Hemispheres red.
5. Color the continent located entirely in the Eastern and Southern Hemispheres green.

Page 25

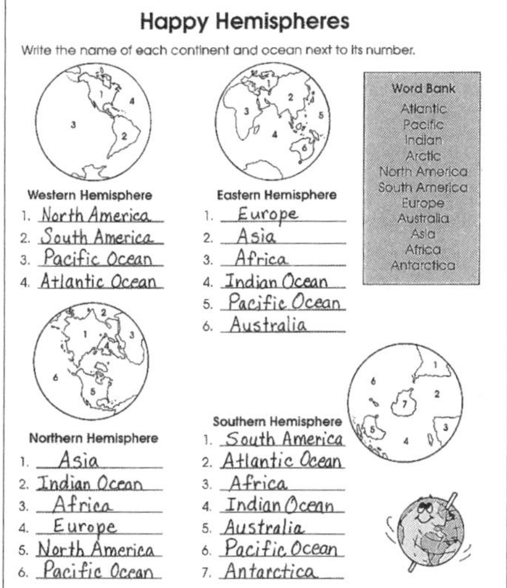

Happy Hemispheres

Write the name of each continent and ocean next to its number.

Word Bank: Atlantic, Pacific, Indian, Arctic, North America, South America, Europe, Australia, Asia, Africa, Antarctica

Western Hemisphere
1. North America
2. South America
3. Pacific Ocean
4. Atlantic Ocean

Eastern Hemisphere
1. Europe
2. Asia
3. Africa
4. Indian Ocean
5. Pacific Ocean
6. Australia

Northern Hemisphere
1. Asia
2. Indian Ocean
3. Africa
4. Europe
5. North America
6. Pacific Ocean

Southern Hemisphere
1. South America
2. Atlantic Ocean
3. Africa
4. Indian Ocean
5. Australia
6. Pacific Ocean
7. Antarctica

Page 26

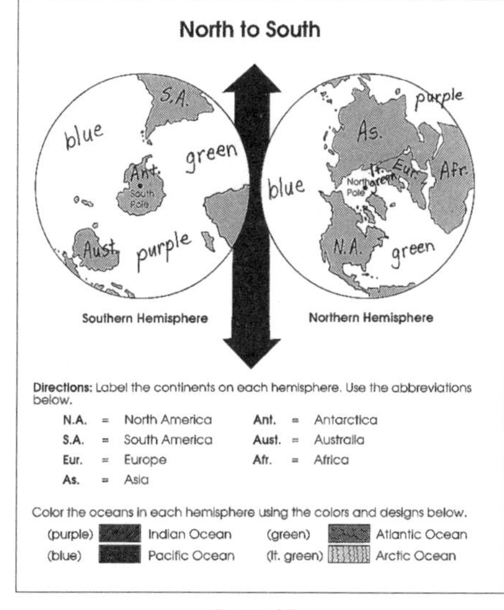

North to South

Directions: Label the continents on each hemisphere. Use the abbreviations below.

N.A. = North America		**Ant.** = Antarctica	
S.A. = South America		**Aust.** = Australia	
Eur. = Europe		**Afr.** = Africa	
As. = Asia			

Color the oceans in each hemisphere using the colors and designs below.

(purple) Indian Ocean (green) Atlantic Ocean
(blue) Pacific Ocean (lt. green) Arctic Ocean

Page 27

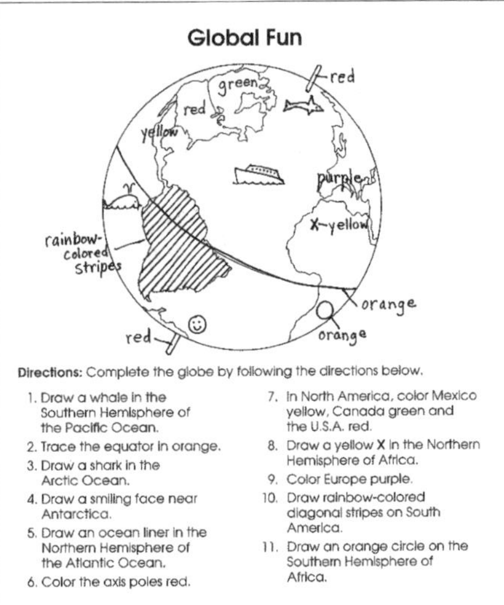

Global Fun

Directions: Complete the globe by following the directions below.

1. Draw a whale in the Southern Hemisphere of the Pacific Ocean.
2. Trace the equator in orange.
3. Draw a shark in the Arctic Ocean.
4. Draw a smiling face near Antarctica.
5. Draw an ocean liner in the Northern Hemisphere of the Atlantic Ocean.
6. Color the axis poles red.
7. In North America, color Mexico yellow, Canada green and the U.S.A. red.
8. Draw a yellow **X** in the Northern Hemisphere of Africa.
9. Color Europe purple.
10. Draw rainbow-colored diagonal stripes on South America.
11. Draw an orange circle on the Southern Hemisphere of Africa.

Page 28

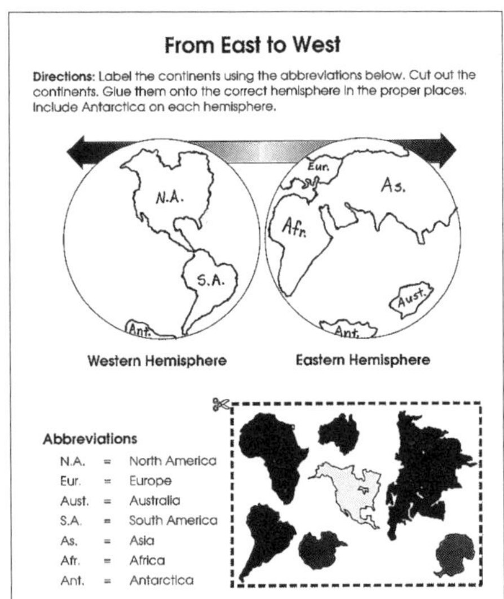

From East to West

Directions: Label the continents using the abbreviations below. Cut out the continents. Glue them onto the correct hemisphere in the proper places. Include Antarctica on each hemisphere.

Abbreviations

N.A. = North America
Eur. = Europe
Aust. = Australia
S.A. = South America
As. = Asia
Afr. = Africa
Ant. = Antarctica

Page 29

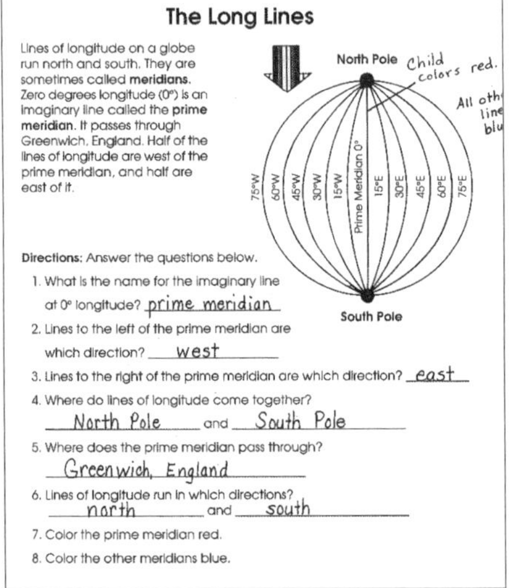

The Long Lines

Lines of longitude on a globe run north and south. They are sometimes called **meridians.** Zero degrees longitude (0°) is an imaginary line called the **prime meridian.** It passes through Greenwich, England. Half of the lines of longitude are west of the prime meridian, and half are east of it.

Directions: Answer the questions below.

1. What is the name for the imaginary line at 0° longitude? prime meridian
2. Lines to the left of the prime meridian are which direction? west
3. Lines to the right of the prime meridian are which direction? east
4. Where do lines of longitude come together? North Pole and South Pole
5. Where does the prime meridian pass through? Greenwich, England
6. Lines of longitude run in which directions? north and south
7. Color the prime meridian red.
8. Color the other meridians blue.

Page 31

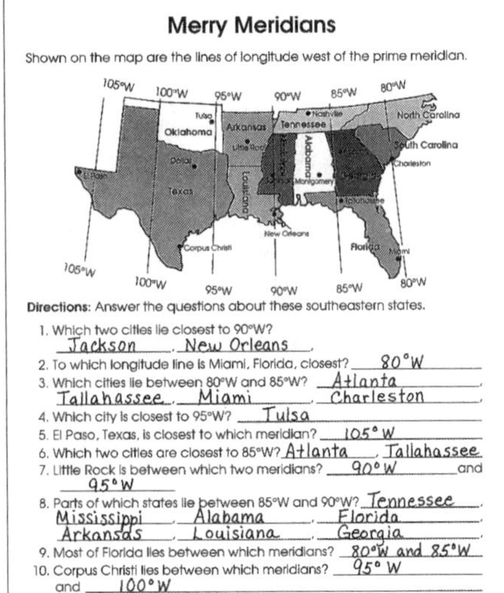

Merry Meridians

Shown on the map are the lines of longitude west of the prime meridian.

Directions: Answer the questions about these southeastern states.

1. Which two cities lie closest to 90°W? Jackson, New Orleans.
2. To which longitude line is Miami, Florida, closest? 80°W
3. Which cities lie between 80°W and 85°W? Atlanta, Tallahassee, Miami, Charleston.
4. Which city is closest to 95°W? Tulsa
5. El Paso, Texas, is closest to which meridian? 105°W
6. Which two cities are closest to 85°W? Atlanta, Tallahassee
7. Little Rock is between which two meridians? 90°W and 95°W
8. Parts of which states lie between 85°W and 90°W? Tennessee, Mississippi, Alabama, Florida, Arkansas, Louisiana, Georgia.
9. Most of Florida lies between which meridians? 80°W and 85°W
10. Corpus Christi lies between which meridians? 95°W and 100°W

Page 32

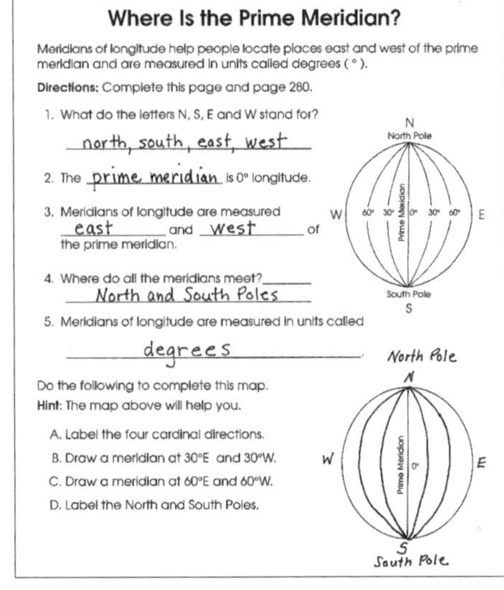

Where Is the Prime Meridian?

Meridians of longitude help people locate places east and west of the prime meridian and are measured in units called degrees (°).

Directions: Complete this page and page 280.

1. What do the letters N, S, E and W stand for? north, south, east, west
2. The prime meridian is 0° longitude.
3. Meridians of longitude are measured east and west of the prime meridian.
4. Where do all the meridians meet? North and South Poles
5. Meridians of longitude are measured in units called degrees.

Do the following to complete this map.
Hint: The map above will help you.

A. Label the four cardinal directions.
B. Draw a meridian at 30°E and 30°W.
C. Draw a meridian at 60°E and 60°W.
D. Label the North and South Poles.

Page 33

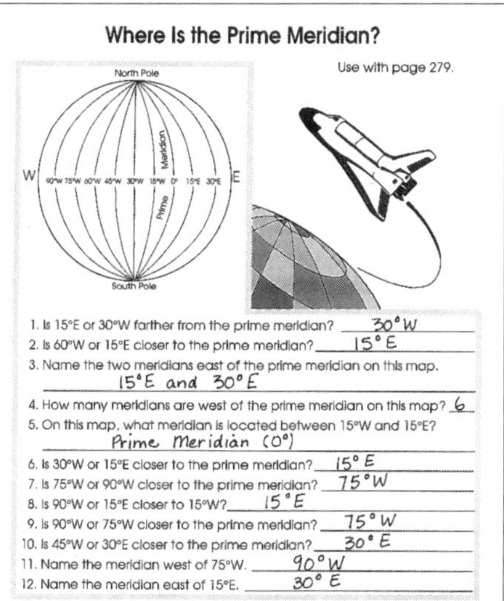

Where Is the Prime Meridian?

Use with page 279.

1. Is 15°E or 30°W farther from the prime meridian? 30° W
2. Is 60°W or 15°E closer to the prime meridian? 15° E
3. Name the two meridians east of the prime meridian on this map. 15° E and 30° E
4. How many meridians are west of the prime meridian on this map? 6
5. On this map, what meridian is located between 15°W and 15°E? Prime Meridian (0°)
6. Is 30°W or 15°E closer to the prime meridian? 15° E
7. Is 75°W or 90°W closer to the prime meridian? 75° W
8. Is 90°W or 15°E closer to 15°W? 15° E
9. Is 90°W or 75°W closer to the prime meridian? 75° W
10. Is 45°W or 30°E closer to the prime meridian? 30° E
11. Name the meridian west of 75°W. 90° W
12. Name the meridian east of 15°E. 30° E

Page 34

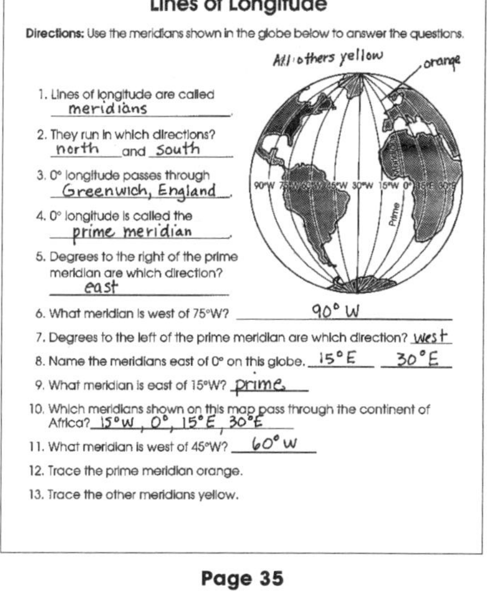

Lines of Longitude

Directions: Use the meridians shown in the globe below to answer the questions.

1. Lines of longitude are called meridians
2. They run in which directions? north and south
3. 0° longitude passes through Greenwich, England.
4. 0° longitude is called the prime meridian
5. Degrees to the right of the prime meridian are which direction? east
6. What meridian is west of 75°W? 90° W
7. Degrees to the left of the prime meridian are which direction? west
8. Name the meridians east of 0° on this globe. 15° E 30° E
9. What meridian is east of 15°W? prime
10. Which meridians shown on this map pass through the continent of Africa? 15° W, 0°, 15° E, 30° E
11. What meridian is west of 45°W? 60° W
12. Trace the prime meridian orange.
13. Trace the other meridians yellow.

Page 35

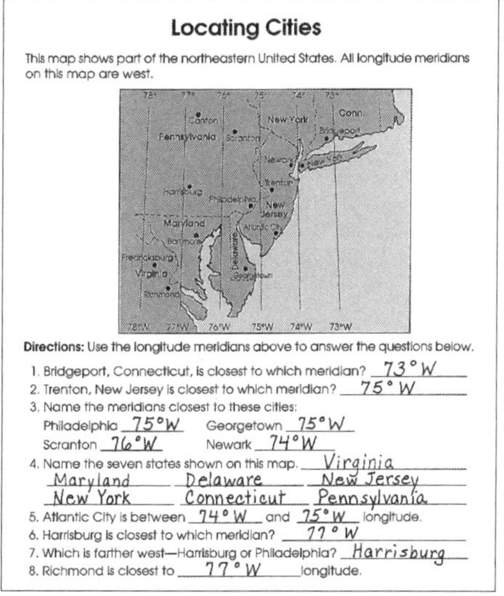

Locating Cities

This map shows part of the northeastern United States. All longitude meridians on this map are west.

Directions: Use the longitude meridians above to answer the questions below.

1. Bridgeport, Connecticut, is closest to which meridian? 73° W
2. Trenton, New Jersey is closest to which meridian? 75° W
3. Name the meridians closest to these cities:
   Philadelphia 75° W Georgetown 75° W
   Scranton 76° W Newark 74° W
4. Name the seven states shown on this map. Virginia, Maryland, Delaware, New Jersey, New York, Connecticut, Pennsylvania
5. Atlantic City is between 74° W and 75° W longitude.
6. Harrisburg is closest to which meridian? 77° W
7. Which is farther west—Harrisburg or Philadelphia? Harrisburg
8. Richmond is closest to 77° W longitude.

Page 36

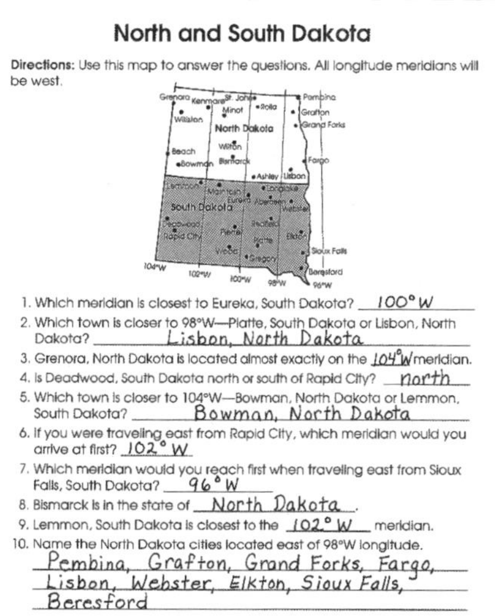

North and South Dakota

Directions: Use this map to answer the questions. All longitude meridians will be west.

1. Which meridian is closest to Eureka, South Dakota? 100° W
2. Which town is closer to 98°W—Platte, South Dakota or Lisbon, North Dakota? Lisbon, North Dakota
3. Grenora, North Dakota is located almost exactly on the 104°W meridian.
4. Is Deadwood, South Dakota north or south of Rapid City? north
5. Which town is closer to 104°W—Bowman, North Dakota or Lemmon, South Dakota? Bowman, North Dakota
6. If you were traveling east from Rapid City, which meridian would you arrive at first? 102° W
7. Which meridian would you reach first when traveling east from Sioux Falls, South Dakota? 96° W
8. Bismarck is in the state of North Dakota.
9. Lemmon, South Dakota is closest to the 102° W meridian.
10. Name the North Dakota cities located east of 98°W longitude. Pembina, Grafton, Grand Forks, Fargo, Lisbon, Webster, Elkton, Sioux Falls, Beresford

Page 37

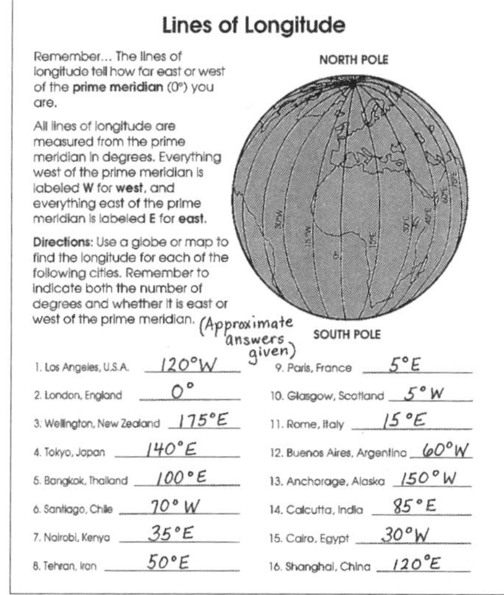

Lines of Longitude

Remember... The lines of longitude tell how far east or west of the **prime meridian** (0°) you are.

All lines of longitude are measured from the prime meridian in degrees. Everything west of the prime meridian is labeled W for **west**, and everything east of the prime meridian is labeled E for **east**.

Directions: Use a globe or map to find the longitude for each of the following cities. Remember to indicate both the number of degrees and whether it is east or west of the prime meridian. (Approximate answers given)

City	Longitude	City	Longitude
1. Los Angeles, U.S.A.	120° W	9. Paris, France	5° E
2. London, England	0°	10. Glasgow, Scotland	5° W
3. Wellington, New Zealand	175° E	11. Rome, Italy	15° E
4. Tokyo, Japan	140° E	12. Buenos Aires, Argentina	60° W
5. Bangkok, Thailand	100° E	13. Anchorage, Alaska	150° W
6. Santiago, Chile	70° W	14. Calcutta, India	85° E
7. Nairobi, Kenya	35° E	15. Cairo, Egypt	30° W
8. Tehran, Iran	50° E	16. Shanghai, China	120° E

Page 38

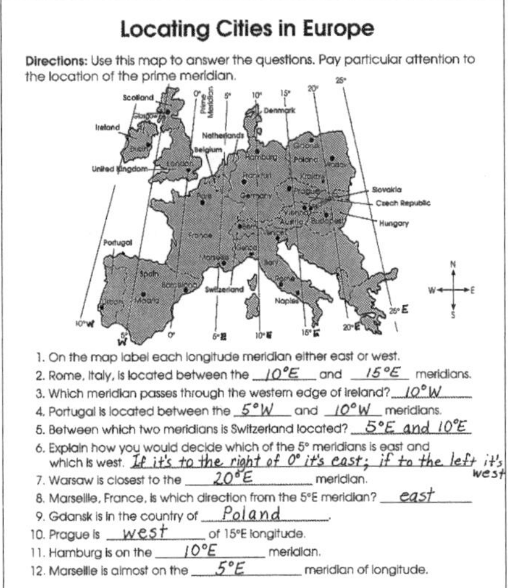

Locating Cities in Europe

Directions: Use this map to answer the questions. Pay particular attention to the location of the prime meridian.

1. On the map label each longitude meridian either east or west.
2. Rome, Italy, is located between the 10°E and 15°E meridians.
3. Which meridian passes through the western edge of Ireland? 10°W
4. Portugal is located between the 5°W and 10°W meridians.
5. Between which two meridians is Switzerland located? 5°E and 10°E
6. Explain how you would decide which of the 5° meridians is east and which is west. If it's to the right of 0° it's east; if to the left it's west
7. Warsaw is closest to the 20°E meridian.
8. Marseille, France, is which direction from the 5°E meridian? east
9. Gdansk is in the country of Poland.
10. Prague is west of 15°E longitude.
11. Hamburg is on the 10°E meridian.
12. Marseille is almost on the 5°E meridian of longitude.

Page 39

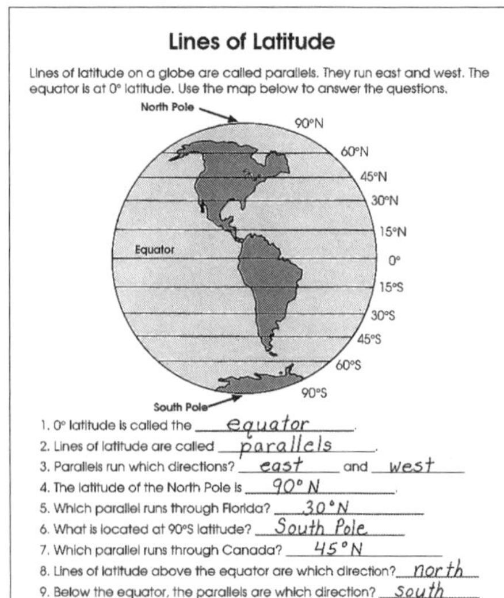

Lines of Latitude

Lines of latitude on a globe are called parallels. They run east and west. The equator is at 0° latitude. Use the map below to answer the questions.

1. 0° latitude is called the equator.
2. Lines of latitude are called parallels.
3. Parallels run which directions? east and west
4. The latitude of the North Pole is 90° N.
5. Which parallel runs through Florida? 30°N
6. What is located at 90°S latitude? South Pole
7. Which parallel runs through Canada? 45°N
8. Lines of latitude above the equator are which direction? north
9. Below the equator, the parallels are which direction? south

Page 40

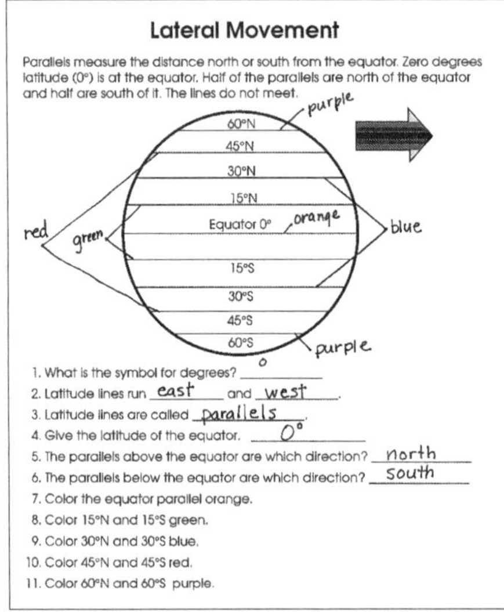

Lateral Movement

Parallels measure the distance north or south from the equator. Zero degrees latitude (0°) is at the equator. Half of the parallels are north of the equator and half are south of it. The lines do not meet.

1. What is the symbol for degrees? °
2. Latitude lines run east and west.
3. Latitude lines are called parallels.
4. Give the latitude of the equator. 0°
5. The parallels above the equator are which direction? north
6. The parallels below the equator are which direction? south
7. Color the equator parallel orange.
8. Color 15°N and 15°S green.
9. Color 30°N and 30°S blue.
10. Color 45°N and 45°S red.
11. Color 60°N and 60°S purple.

Page 41

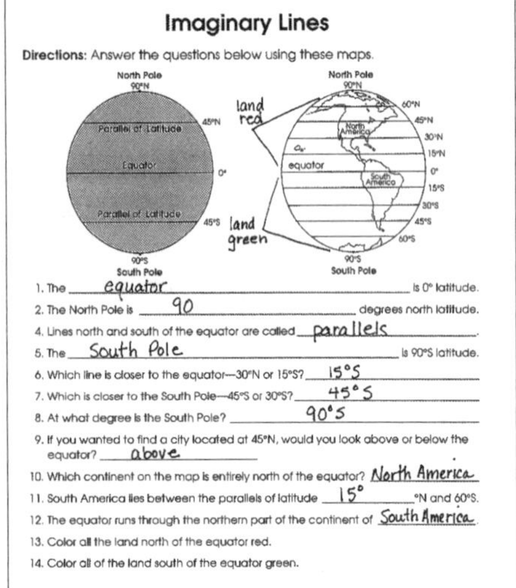

Imaginary Lines

Directions: Answer the questions below using these maps.

1. The equator is 0° latitude.
2. The North Pole is 90 degrees north latitude.
4. Lines north and south of the equator are called parallels.
5. The South Pole is 90°S latitude.
6. Which line is closer to the equator—30°N or 15°S? 15°S
7. Which is closer to the South Pole—45°S or 30°S? 45°S
8. At what degree is the South Pole? 90°S
9. If you wanted to find a city located at 45°N, would you look above or below the equator? above
10. Which continent on the map is entirely north of the equator? North America
11. South America lies between the parallels of latitude 15° °N and 60°S.
12. The equator runs through the northern part of the continent of South America
13. Color all the land north of the equator red.
14. Color all of the land south of the equator green.

Page 42

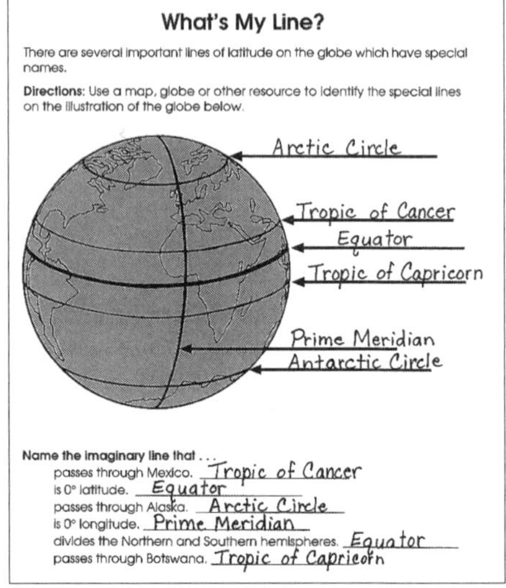

What's My Line?

There are several important lines of latitude on the globe which have special names.

Directions: Use a map, globe or other resource to identify the special lines on the illustration of the globe below.

Name the imaginary line that . . .

passes through Mexico. Tropic of Cancer
is 0° latitude. Equator
passes through Alaska. Arctic Circle
is 0° longitude. Prime Meridian
divides the Northern and Southern hemispheres. Equator
passes through Botswana. Tropic of Capricorn

Page 43

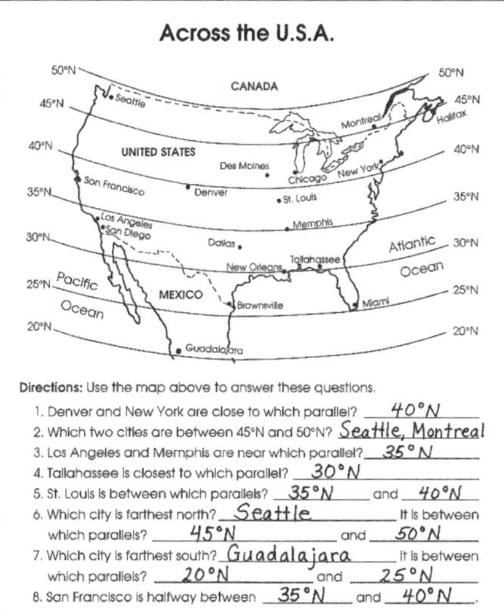

Across the U.S.A.

Directions: Use the map above to answer these questions.

1. Denver and New York are close to which parallel? 40°N
2. Which two cities are between 45°N and 50°N? Seattle, Montreal
3. Los Angeles and Memphis are near which parallel? 35°N
4. Tallahassee is closest to which parallel? 30°N
5. St. Louis is between which parallels? 35°N and 40°N
6. Which city is farthest north? Seattle It is between which parallels? 45°N and 50°N
7. Which city is farthest south? Guadalajara It is between which parallels? 20°N and 25°N
8. San Francisco is halfway between 35°N and 40°N.

Page 44

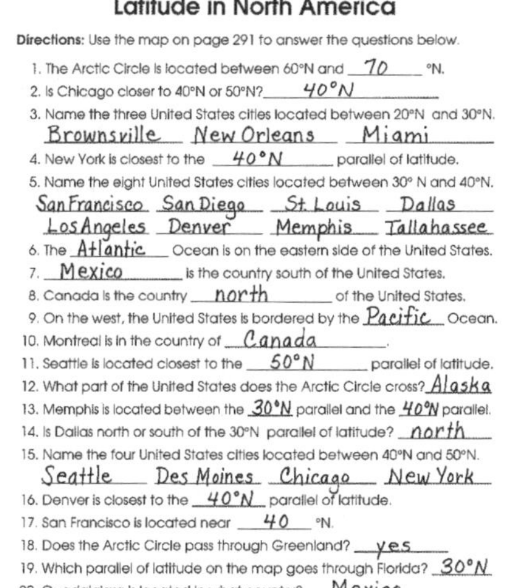

Latitude in North America

Directions: Use the map on page 291 to answer the questions below.

1. The Arctic Circle is located between 60°N and 70 °N.
2. Is Chicago closer to 40°N or 50°N? 40°N
3. Name the three United States cities located between 20°N and 30°N. Brownsville New Orleans Miami
4. New York is closest to the 40°N parallel of latitude.
5. Name the eight United States cities located between 30° N and 40°N. San Francisco San Diego St. Louis Dallas Los Angeles Denver Memphis Tallahassee
6. The Atlantic Ocean is on the eastern side of the United States.
7. Mexico is the country south of the United States.
8. Canada is the country north of the United States.
9. On the west, the United States is bordered by the Pacific Ocean.
10. Montreal is in the country of Canada.
11. Seattle is located closest to the 50°N parallel of latitude.
12. What part of the United States does the Arctic Circle cross? Alaska
13. Memphis is located between the 30°N parallel and the 40°N parallel.
14. Is Dallas north or south of the 30°N parallel of latitude? north
15. Name the four United States cities located between 40°N and 50°N. Seattle Des Moines Chicago New York
16. Denver is closest to the 40°N parallel of latitude.
17. San Francisco is located near 40 °N.
18. Does the Arctic Circle pass through Greenland? yes
19. Which parallel of latitude on the map goes through Florida? 30°N
20. Guadalajara is located in what country? Mexico

Page 46

Parallels Help With Location

1. Billings, Montana is which direction from the 46°N parallel? south
2. Pueblo, Colorado is almost directly on the 38°N parallel of latitude.
3. The boundary between Oregon and California is formed by the 42°N parallel.
4. The state of Wyoming is located between 41°N parallel and 45°N parallel.
5. Name three cities in Idaho south of the 45°N parallel of latitude. Idaho Falls Boise Pocatello
6. Which of these cities is south of the 35°N parallel—Flagstaff, Arizona or Roswell, New Mexico? Roswell, New Mexico
7. Name the three California cities located between the 35°N and 38°N parallels. Stockton Fresno San Francisco
8. All of the cities shown in Washington are between the parallels of 46°N and 47°N.
9. Which two Nevada cities are north of the 38°N parallel? Reno and Elko
10. Klamath Falls, Oregon is almost directly on the 42°N parallel.

Page 47

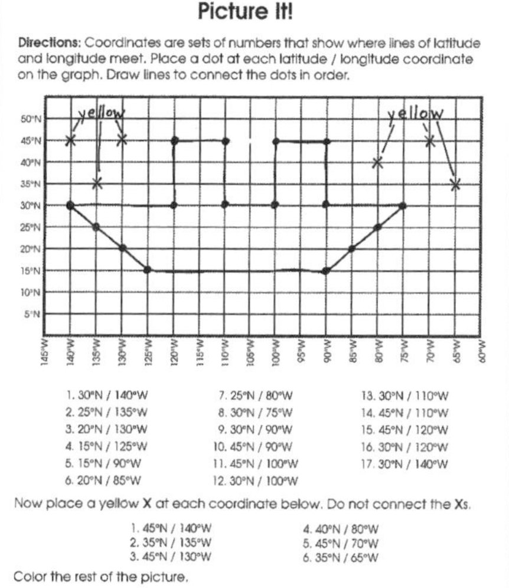

Picture It!

Directions: Coordinates are sets of numbers that show where lines of latitude and longitude meet. Place a dot at each latitude / longitude coordinate on the graph. Draw lines to connect the dots in order.

1. 30°N / 140°W
2. 25°N / 135°W
3. 20°N / 130°W
4. 15°N / 125°W
5. 15°N / 90°W
6. 20°N / 85°W
7. 25°N / 80°W
8. 30°N / 75°W
9. 30°N / 90°W
10. 45°N / 90°W
11. 45°N / 100°W
12. 30°N / 100°W
13. 30°N / 110°W
14. 45°N / 110°W
15. 45°N / 120°W
16. 30°N / 120°W
17. 30°N / 140°W

Now place a yellow **X** at each coordinate below. Do not connect the Xs.

1. 45°N / 140°W
2. 35°N / 135°W
3. 45°N / 130°W
4. 40°N / 80°W
5. 45°N / 70°W
6. 35°N / 65°W

Color the rest of the picture.

Page 48

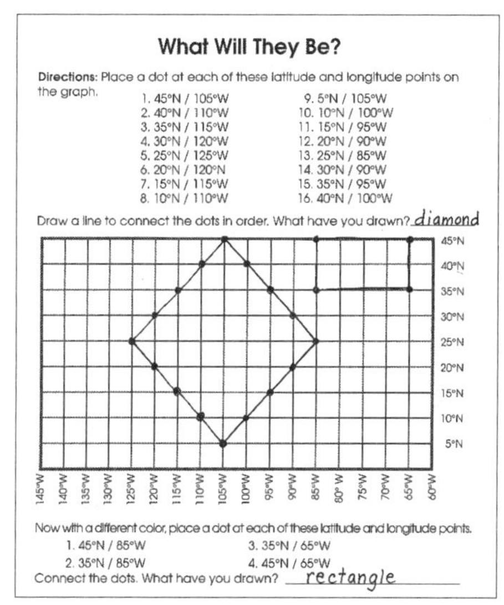

What Will They Be?

Directions: Place a dot at each of these latitude and longitude points on the graph.

1. 45°N / 105°W
2. 40°N / 110°W
3. 35°N / 115°W
4. 30°N / 120°W
5. 25°N / 125°W
6. 20°N / 120°W
7. 15°N / 115°W
8. 10°N / 110°W
9. 5°N / 105°W
10. 10°N / 100°W
11. 15°N / 95°W
12. 20°N / 90°W
13. 25°N / 85°W
14. 30°N / 90°W
15. 35°N / 95°W
16. 40°N / 100°W

Draw a line to connect the dots in order. What have you drawn? diamond

Now with a different color, place a dot at each of these latitude and longitude points.

1. 45°N / 85°W
2. 35°N / 85°W
3. 35°N / 65°W
4. 45°N / 65°W

Connect the dots. What have you drawn? rectangle

Page 49

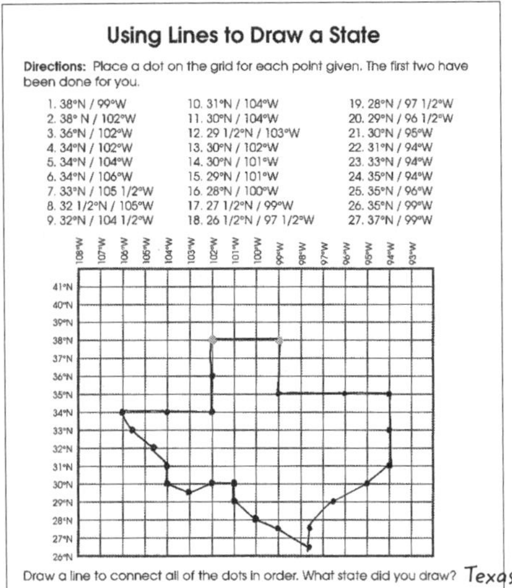

Using Lines to Draw a State

Directions: Place a dot on the grid for each point given. The first two have been done for you.

1. 38°N / 99°W	10. 31°N / 104°W	19. 28°N / 97 1/2°W
2. 38° N / 102°W	11. 30°N / 104°W	20. 29°N / 96 1/2°W
3. 36°N / 102°W	12. 29 1/2°N / 103°W	21. 30°N / 95°W
4. 34°N / 102°W	13. 30°N / 102°W	22. 31°N / 94°W
5. 34°N / 104°W	14. 30°N / 101°W	23. 33°N / 94°W
6. 34°N / 106°W	15. 29°N / 101°W	24. 35°N / 94°W
7. 33°N / 105 1/2°W	16. 28°N / 100°W	25. 35°N / 96°W
8. 32 1/2°N / 105°W	17. 27 1/2°N / 99°W	26. 35°N / 99°W
9. 32°N / 104 1/2°W	18. 26 1/2°N / 97 1/2°W	27. 37°N / 99°W

Draw a line to connect all of the dots in order. What state did you draw? Texas

Page 50

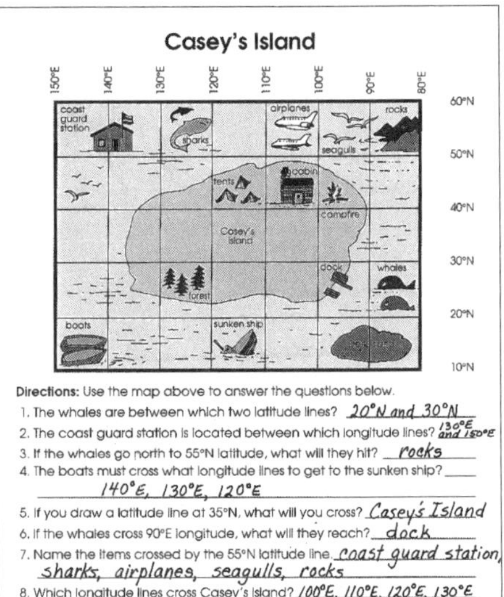

Casey's Island

Directions: Use the map above to answer the questions below.

1. The whales are between which two latitude lines? 20°N and 30°N
2. The coast guard station is located between which longitude lines? 130°E and 150°E
3. If the whales go north to 55°N latitude, what will they hit? rocks
4. The boats must cross what longitude lines to get to the sunken ship? 140°E, 130°E, 120°E
5. If you draw a latitude line at 35°N, what will you cross? Casey's Island
6. If the whales cross 90°E longitude, what will they reach? dock
7. Name the items crossed by the 55°N latitude line. coast guard station, sharks, airplanes, seagulls, rocks
8. Which longitude lines cross Casey's Island? 100°E, 110°E, 120°E, 130°E

Page 51

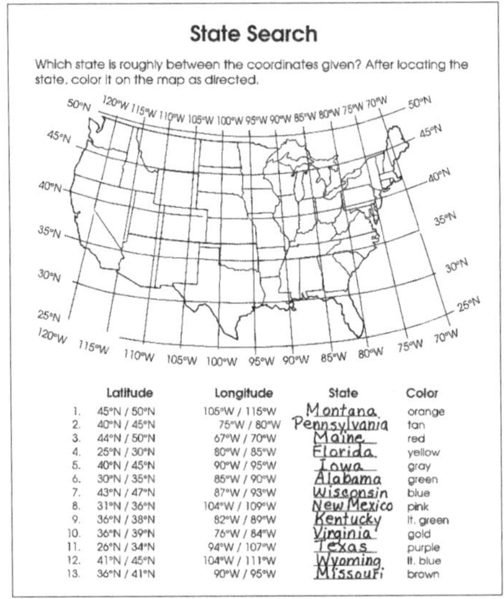

State Search

Which state is roughly between the coordinates given? After locating the state, color it on the map as directed.

	Latitude	Longitude	State	Color
1.	45°N / 50°N	105°W / 115°W	Montana	orange
2.	40°N / 45°N	75°W / 80°W	Pennsylvania	tan
3.	44°N / 50°N	67°W / 70°W	Maine	red
4.	25°N / 30°N	80°W / 85°W	Florida	yellow
5.	40°N / 45°N	90°W / 95°W	Iowa	gray
6.	30°N / 35°N	85°W / 90°W	Alabama	green
7.	43°N / 47°N	87°W / 93°W	Wisconsin	blue
8.	31°N / 36°N	104°W / 109°W	New Mexico	pink
9.	36°N / 38°N	82°W / 89°W	Kentucky	lt. green
10.	36°N / 39°N	76°W / 84°W	Virginia	gold
11.	26°N / 34°N	94°W / 107°W	Texas	purple
12.	41°N / 45°N	104°W / 111°W	Wyoming	lt. blue
13.	36°N / 41°N	90°W / 95°W	Missouri	brown

Page 52

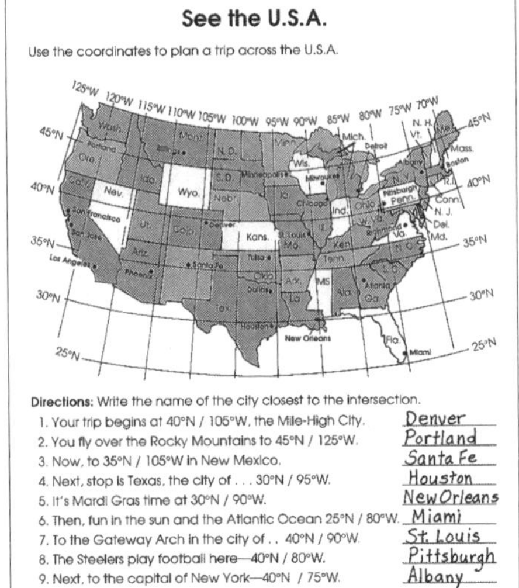

See the U.S.A.

Use the coordinates to plan a trip across the U.S.A.

Directions: Write the name of the city closest to the intersection.

1. Your trip begins at 40°N / 105°W, the Mile-High City. Denver
2. You fly over the Rocky Mountains to 45°N / 125°W. Portland
3. Now, to 35°N / 105°W in New Mexico. Santa Fe
4. Next, stop is Texas, the city of . . . 30°N / 95°W. Houston
5. It's Mardi Gras time at 30°N / 90°W. New Orleans
6. Then, fun in the sun and the Atlantic Ocean 25°N / 80°W. Miami
7. To the Gateway Arch in the city of . . 40°N / 90°W. St. Louis
8. The Steelers play football here—40°N / 80°W. Pittsburgh
9. Next, to the capital of New York—40°N / 75°W. Albany

Page 53

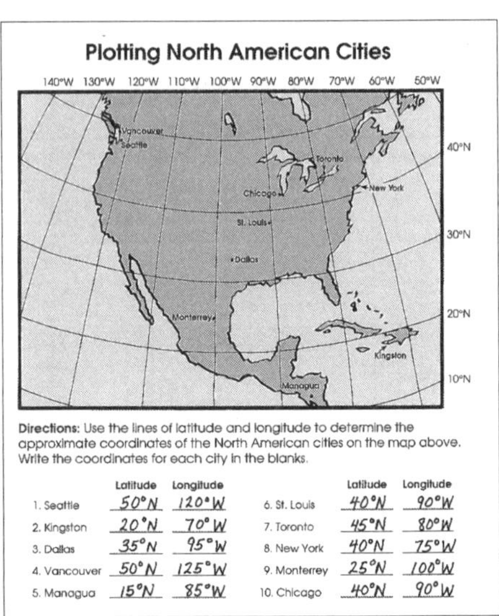

Plotting North American Cities

Directions: Use the lines of latitude and longitude to determine the approximate coordinates of the North American cities on the map above. Write the coordinates for each city in the blanks.

	Latitude	Longitude		Latitude	Longitude
1. Seattle	50°N	120°W	6. St. Louis	40°N	90°W
2. Kingston	20°N	70°W	7. Toronto	45°N	80°W
3. Dallas	35°N	95°W	8. New York	40°N	75°W
4. Vancouver	50°N	125°W	9. Monterrey	25°N	100°W
5. Managua	15°N	85°W	10. Chicago	40°N	90°W

Page 54

Batter Up!

Directions: Use the coordinates below and the map on page 302 to locate these cities. Then, unscramble the words to find out the baseball teams which call these cities "home base."

	Latitude	Longitude	City	State	Baseball Team Names		
1.	41°N	74°W	New York City	NY	(yeesank) or (tmes)	=	Yankees (or Mets)
2.	40°N	105°W	Denver	CO	(ocrkeis)	=	Rockies
3.	34°N	84°W	Atlanta	GA	(sebarv)	=	Braves
4.	29°N	96°W	Houston	TX	(satosr)	=	Astros
5.	39°N	84°W	Cincinnati	OH	(dser)	=	Reds
6.	38°N	123°W	San Francisco	CA	(ginsta)	=	Giants
7.	42°N	88°W	Chicago	IL	(cbus) or (twihe xso)	=	Cubs (or White Sox)
8.	47°N	122°W	Seattle	WA	(raimnesr)	=	Mariners
9.	39°N	90°W	St. Louis	MO	(rdcailnas)	=	Cardinals
10.	42°N	82°W	Cleveland	OH	(nidaisn)	=	Indians
11.	43°N	71°W	Boston	MA	(der sxo)	=	Red Sox
12.	34°N	117°W	Los Angeles	CA	(ddogesr)	=	Dodgers
13.	39°N	76°W	Baltimore	MD	(rioolse)	=	Orioles

Word Bank: Orioles, Indians, Cardinals, Dodgers, Giants, Rockies, Cubs, White Sox, Yankees, Astros, Mets, Braves, Reds, Mariners, Red Sox

Page 55

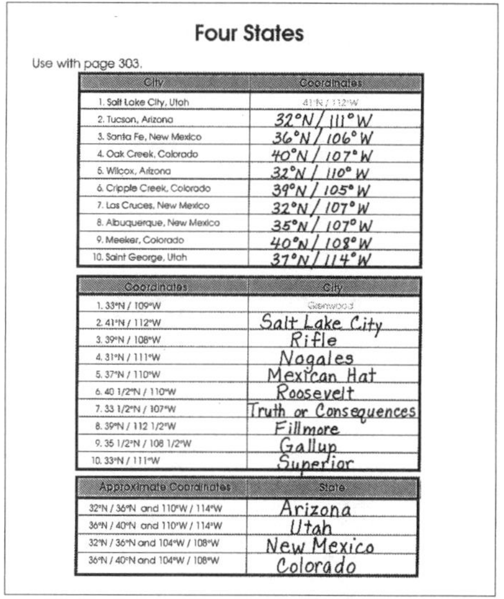

Four States

Use with page 303.

City	Coordinates
1. Salt Lake City, Utah	41°N / 112°W
2. Tucson, Arizona	32°N / 111°W
3. Santa Fe, New Mexico	36°N / 106°W
4. Oak Creek, Colorado	40°N / 107°W
5. Wilcox, Arizona	32°N / 110°W
6. Cripple Creek, Colorado	39°N / 105°W
7. Las Cruces, New Mexico	32°N / 107°W
8. Albuquerque, New Mexico	35°N / 107°W
9. Meeker, Colorado	40°N / 108°W
10. Saint George, Utah	37°N / 114°W

Coordinates	City
1. 33°N / 109°W	Glenwood
2. 41°N / 112°W	Salt Lake City
3. 39°N / 108°W	Rifle
4. 31°N / 111°W	Nogales
5. 37°N / 110°W	Mexican Hat
6. 40 1/2°N / 110°W	Roosevelt
7. 33 1/2°N / 107°W	Truth or Consequences
8. 39°N / 112 1/2°W	Fillmore
9. 35 1/2°N / 108 1/2°W	Gallup
10. 33°N / 111°W	Superior

Approximate Coordinates	State
32°N / 36°N and 110°W / 114°W	Arizona
36°N / 40°N and 110°W / 114°W	Utah
32°N / 36°N and 104°W / 108°W	New Mexico
36°N / 40°N and 104°W / 108°W	Colorado

Page 58

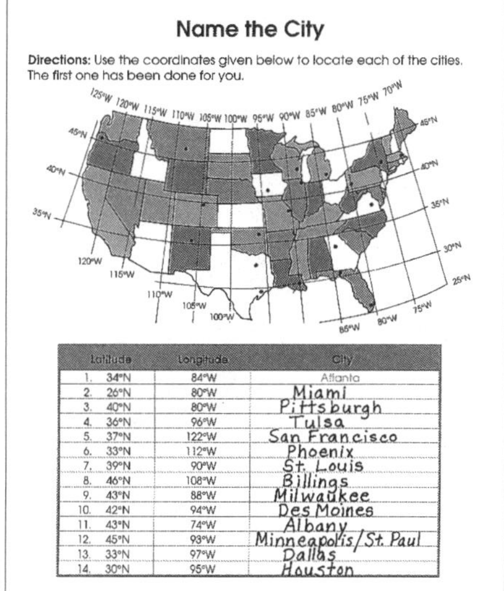

Name the City

Directions: Use the coordinates given below to locate each of the cities. The first one has been done for you.

	Latitude	Longitude	City
1.	34°N	84°W	Atlanta
2.	26°N	80°W	Miami
3.	40°N	80°W	Pittsburgh
4.	36°N	96°W	Tulsa
5.	37°N	122°W	San Francisco
6.	33°N	112°W	Phoenix
7.	39°N	90°W	St. Louis
8.	46°N	108°W	Billings
9.	43°N	88°W	Milwaukee
10.	42°N	94°W	Des Moines
11.	43°N	74°W	Albany
12.	45°N	93°W	Minneapolis/St. Paul
13.	33°N	97°W	Dallas
14.	30°N	95°W	Houston

Page 59

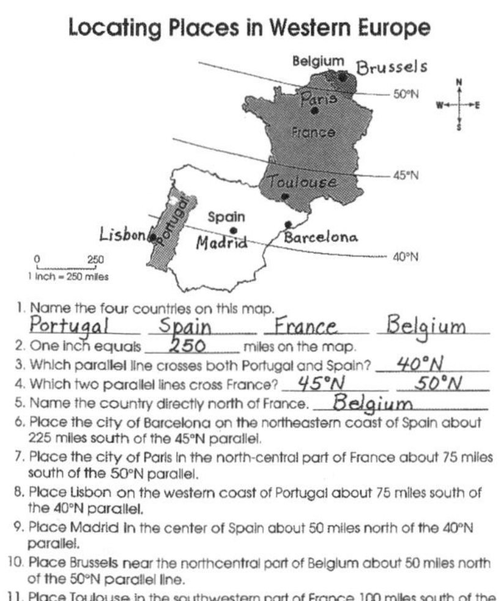

Locating Places in Western Europe

1. Name the four countries on this map. Portugal Spain France Belgium
2. One inch equals 250 miles on the map.
3. Which parallel line crosses both Portugal and Spain? 40°N
4. Which two parallel lines cross France? 45°N 50°N
5. Name the country directly north of France. Belgium
6. Place the city of Barcelona on the northeastern coast of Spain about 225 miles south of the 45°N parallel.
7. Place the city of Paris in the north-central part of France about 75 miles south of the 50°N parallel.
8. Place Lisbon on the western coast of Portugal about 75 miles south of the 40°N parallel.
9. Place Madrid in the center of Spain about 50 miles north of the 40°N parallel.
10. Place Brussels near the northcentral part of Belgium about 50 miles north of the 50°N parallel line.
11. Place Toulouse in the southwestern part of France 100 miles south of the 45°N parallel.

Page 60

Where in Europe?

Directions: Estimate and write the coordinates and countries for these European cities using the map on page 307. The first one has been done for you.

City	Latitude	Longitude	Country
1. London	52°N	0°	United Kingdom
2. Belgrade	45°N	20°E	Yugoslavia
3. Warsaw	57°N	21°E	Poland
4. Stockholm	59°N	18°E	Sweden
5. Athens	38°N	23°E	Greece
6. Helsinki	61°N	25°E	Finland
7. Paris	48°N	3°E	France
8. Munich	47°N	12°E	Germany
9. Copenhagen	56°N	13°E	Denmark
10. Oslo	60°N	11°E	Norway
11. Glasgow	56°N	6°E	United Kingdom
12. Prague	50°N	14°E	Czech Republic
13. Bern	47°N	8°E	Switzerland
14. Hamburg	53°N	10°E	Germany
15. Dresden	52°N	13°E	Germany
16. Dublin	53°N	6°W	Ireland
17. Rome	42°N	13°E	Italy
18. Budapest	43°N	18°E	Hungary
19. Vienna	48°N	16°E	Austria
20. Amsterdam	53°N	5°E	Netherlands

Page 62

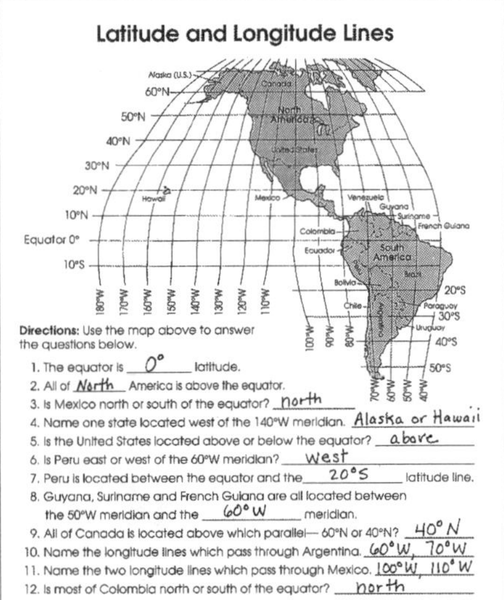

Latitude and Longitude Lines

Directions: Use the map above to answer the questions below.

1. The equator is ___0°___ latitude.
2. All of ___North___ America is above the equator.
3. Is Mexico north or south of the equator? ___north___
4. Name one state located west of the 140°W meridian. ___Alaska or Hawaii___
5. Is the United States located above or below the equator? ___above___
6. Is Peru east or west of the 60°W meridian? ___west___
7. Peru is located between the equator and the ___20°S___ latitude line.
8. Guyana, Suriname and French Guiana are all located between the 50°W meridian and the ___60°W___ meridian.
9. All of Canada is located above which parallel— 60°N or 40°N? ___40°N___
10. Name the longitude lines which pass through Argentina. ___60°W, 70°W___
11. Name the two longitude lines which pass through Mexico. ___100°W, 110°W___
12. Is most of Colombia north or south of the equator? ___north___

Page 63

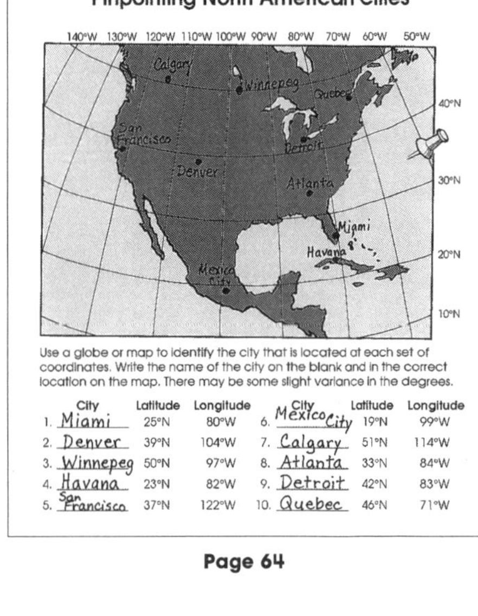

Pinpointing North American Cities

Use a globe or map to identify the city that is located at each set of coordinates. Write the name of the city on the blank and in the correct location on the map. There may be some slight variance in the degrees.

City	Latitude	Longitude	City	Latitude	Longitude
1. Miami	25°N	80°W	6. Mexico City	19°N	99°W
2. Denver	39°N	104°W	7. Calgary	51°N	114°W
3. Winnepeg	50°N	97°W	8. Atlanta	33°N	84°W
4. Havana	23°N	82°W	9. Detroit	42°N	83°W
5. San Francisco	37°N	122°W	10. Quebec	46°N	71°W

Page 64

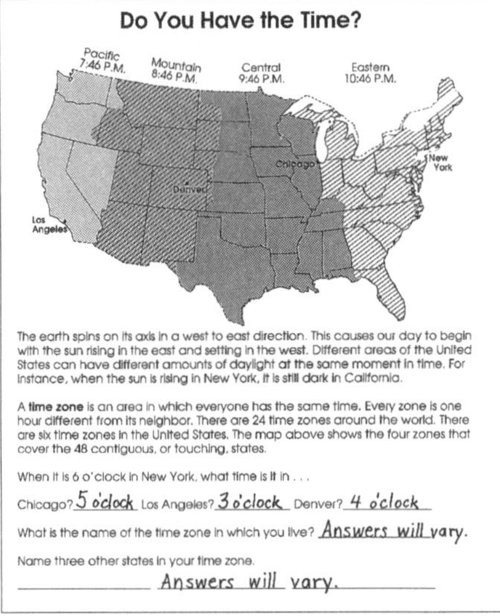

Do You Have the Time?

The earth spins on its axis in a west to east direction. This causes our day to begin with the sun rising in the east and setting in the west. Different areas of the United States can have different amounts of daylight at the same moment in time. For instance, when the sun is rising in New York, it is still dark in California.

A **time zone** is an area in which everyone has the same time. Every zone is one hour different from its neighbor. There are 24 time zones around the world. There are six time zones in the United States. The map above shows the four zones that cover the 48 contiguous, or touching, states.

When it is 6 o'clock in New York, what time is it in . . .

Chicago? ___5 o'clock___ Los Angeles? ___3 o'clock___ Denver? ___4 o'clock___

What is the name of the time zone in which you live? ___Answers will vary.___

Name three other states in your time zone.

___Answers will vary.___

Page 66

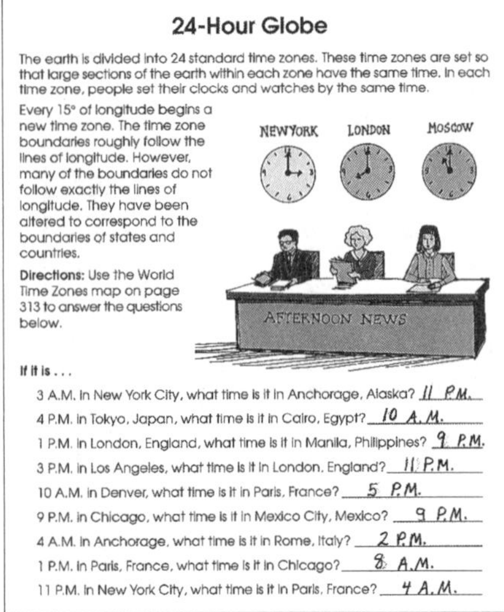

24-Hour Globe

The earth is divided into 24 standard time zones. These time zones are set so that large sections of the earth within each zone have the same time. In each time zone, people set their clocks and watches by the same time.

Every 15° of longitude begins a new time zone. The time zone boundaries roughly follow the lines of longitude. However, many of the boundaries do not follow exactly the lines of longitude. They have been altered to correspond to the boundaries of states and countries.

Directions: Use the World Time Zones map on page 313 to answer the questions below.

If it is . . .

3 A.M. in New York City, what time is it in Anchorage, Alaska? ___11 P.M.___

4 P.M. in Tokyo, Japan, what time is it in Cairo, Egypt? ___10 A.M.___

1 P.M. in London, England, what time is it in Manila, Philippines? ___9 P.M.___

3 P.M. in Los Angeles, what time is it in London, England? ___11 P.M.___

10 A.M. in Denver, what time is it in Paris, France? ___5 P.M.___

9 P.M. in Chicago, what time is it in Mexico City, Mexico? ___9 P.M.___

4 A.M. in Anchorage, what time is it in Rome, Italy? ___2 P.M.___

1 P.M. in Paris, France, what time is it in Chicago? ___8 A.M.___

11 P.M. in New York City, what time is it in Paris, France? ___4 A.M.___

Page 68

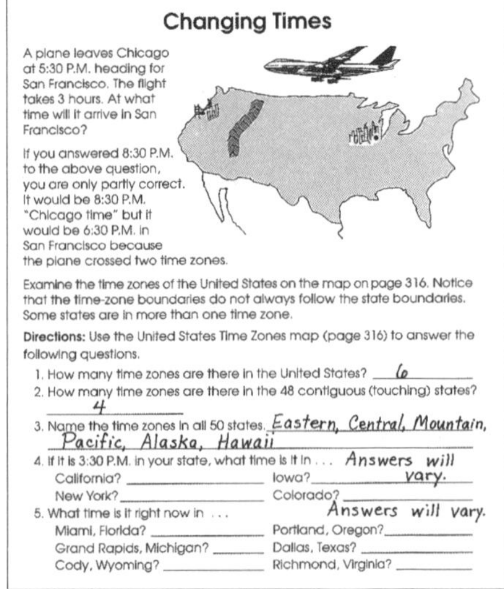

Changing Times

A plane leaves Chicago at 5:30 P.M. heading for San Francisco. The flight takes 3 hours. At what time will it arrive in San Francisco?

If you answered 8:30 P.M. to the above question, you are only partly correct. It would be 8:30 P.M. "Chicago time" but it would be 6:30 P.M. in San Francisco because the plane crossed two time zones.

Examine the time zones of the United States on the map on page 316. Notice that the time-zone boundaries do not always follow the state boundaries. Some states are in more than one time zone.

Directions: Use the United States Time Zones map (page 316) to answer the following questions.

1. How many time zones are there in the United States? ___6___
2. How many time zones are there in the 48 contiguous (touching) states? ___4___
3. Name the time zones in all 50 states. ___Eastern, Central, Mountain, Pacific, Alaska, Hawaii___
4. If it is 3:30 P.M. in your state, what time is it in . . . ___Answers will vary.___
   California? ______ Iowa? ______
   New York? ______ Colorado? ______
5. What time is it right now in . . . ___Answers will vary.___
   Miami, Florida? ______ Portland, Oregon? ______
   Grand Rapids, Michigan? ______ Dallas, Texas? ______
   Cody, Wyoming? ______ Richmond, Virginia? ______

Page 69

